ROTHSCHILD
on
ANTIQUES
&
COLLECTIBLES

ROTHSCHILD
on
ANTIQUES
&
COLLECTIBLES
A Practical Guide to Collecting

SIGMUND ROTHSCHILD

with

RENI L. WITT

World Almanac Publications   New York, New York

Interior design: Levavi & Levavi
Cover design: Robert Anthony, Inc.

First published in 1986

Distributed in the United States by Ballantine Books, a division of Random
House, Inc. and in Canada by Random House of Canada, Ltd.

Library of Congress Catalog Card Number: 85-051937
Newspaper Enterprise Association ISBN 0-911818-92-8
Ballantine Books ISBN 0-345-33410-8

Printed in the United States of America
World Almanac Publications
Newspaper Enterprise Association
A division of United Media Enterprises
A Scripps-Howard Company
200 Park Avenue
New York, NY 10166

Dedicated to my very capable assistants, particularly Jane Ashlock Harris and Libby Crane, Ph.D., as well as Rita Weaver and Diane Warren, and all my other loyal friends that contributed reminiscences in one way or another to this volume.

Contents

ROTHSCHILD
on
ANTIQUES
&
COLLECTIBLES

CHAPTER ONE

Everybody Has Something of Value

"Sigmund Rothschild?"

"Speaking."

"I have a collection I'd like appraised."

"Fine. What is it?"

"Well, I'd rather not say over the phone. Can you come to my farm in Illinois to do an appraisal for insurance?"

"What is it you want appraised?"

The man evaded my question. Piqued with curiosity, I agreed to meet him at the O'Hare Airport. He drove many miles south and went into the farm country. Finally at dusk, we arrived. He pointed to a large red barn and said, "It's in there."

I was most eager to have a look at this mysterious collection, but my host hesitated and seemed rather embarrassed. He said, "It's late. Get a good night's rest and we'll go out early tomorrow morning."

1

Shortly after sunrise, and breakfast, my host led me to an enormous barn and ushered me inside. There, in front of me stood over 100 outhouses and 100 cast iron stoves.

Where he got them, and how he got them there, makes for many stories. This was his hobby—collecting outhouses. All were clean, in good condition, stylistically interesting, and some were even amusing.

I worked all day, examining and appraising each one. He thanked me and I thought, "This confirms what I have always believed: *Anything made by God or man is collected by someone.*"

Everyone has something he is curious about that may have some value. It may be long forgotten in the attic or buried in the basement; it may be proudly displayed in the home or collecting dust in a desk drawer, but almost everybody has something of value, something that is collectible.

Collecting is a human impulse. There is a desire for possession, the search for identification that is often gratified by collecting. Collecting is a fascinating and enjoyable way to create your own world, one which you own and control.

A collection can consist of traditional items—furniture, silver, glassware, paintings; or it can be made up of unusual things—Civil War binoculars, theatrical posters, photographs, bronze nudes, Elvis Presley memorabilia, even baseball cards.

I know. I've appraised just about every type of thing that's ever been collected, including some of the greatest private art collections and important museum collections in the world, as well as that assemblage of outhouses and herd of elephants.

The demand for the unusual collectible is greater than most people realize—and so is the potential for profit. If you make the right buying decisions, your collection can increase in value in a relatively short time. With a little bit of luck, and an intelligent approach to the marketplace, the value of your investment might increase from 50% to 500% over your cost in just a few years.

How can you determine value and make those crucial correct choices? Let's face it, most people who collect become intensely *passionate* about their particular specialty. They also may buy on impulse because they like something—they simply want to own it. Don't forget, collectors are creating their own world.

Needless to say, there is a great deal of emotion involved when

EVERYBODY HAS SOMETHING OF VALUE

buying or selling antiques, art, and collectibles. But buying on emotion does not always result in getting the best value. How do you go about balancing the emotional, or sensual, approach to collecting with the intellectual, or sensible, approach?

The key word is *balance*. Collecting wisely or for profit is neither dull nor cold-blooded. Instead, it is fun; there should be the thrill of possessing something that's beautiful and is of real value. By learning about perfection, age, style, and taste, you can enhance the sensuous aspect of collecting while developing your sensible purchasing and profit-making technique.

This is the basic premise of this book. I hope to share with you my ideas on value, quality, line, form, and color as well as how to recognize them. I also plan to delve into ethics, honesty, business, and law as they relate to collecting. And you'll learn how to use these concepts in the very real world of antique shops, auctions, estate sales, and even flea markets.

These pages, in other words, are the sum total of my years as an appraiser. Measuring value has been my business for almost four decades. Since I started, I have appraised a wide variety of art objects and antiques of unique and varied character. I have appraised important collections for many rich and famous people, but most of the things I see are ordinary, everyday items owned by not-so-well-known individuals. This has given me a particularly advantageous overview of the antique, art, and general market.

This insight did not develop overnight, even though I grew up in the antique business. My father was an antique dealer and an active professional hobbyist. This early exposure sparked an interest that has only intensified with time. I might have become a dealer, except for my personal career ideal. As a young man, I wanted only to be a sculptor creating monumental works of art. My early art education was spurred by this goal, which turned out to be the best schooling for developing perception of form, color, and physical materials—all of which I find are invaluable to the appraiser. Even today, when I look at any work of art, antique piece, or collectible item, my first reaction is sensory rather than intellectual. But I follow up by reinforcing that first reaction with knowledge backed by sound research.

Unfortunately, my first career as a sculptor came to an end when I married and started a family. In order to earn a living and still use what I learned in training, I turned to restoring art and antiques. This turned out to be an important step in my becoming an appraiser.

Restoration is very hard work that takes enormous patience. A restorer has to know materials. He needs a sound understanding of chemistry. He has to know artistic periods and the effects of time. And he must have an excellent eye for and skill in applying color. This work became the basis for what would ultimately become my major vocation—that of appraising.

People frequently asked me the value of a piece I'd restored for them. Since I had no specific training as yet in determining value, this became a necessary part of my learning process. As time passed, the question of value began to intrigue me more and more. After World War II, I was able to continue my education in art, antiques, and collectibles, and so I eased into the field of appraising.

Appraising holds great appeal for me because it presents a broader scope than restoration. As a restorer, my world was concentrated on the one piece I was working on. My days were spent sitting in front of the table or easel giving full concentration to the work being repaired or restored. I needed to expand my horizons and found that appraising was a greater, more stimulating challenge—part of a more exciting life. As a result, I've met many interesting people and have had the opportunity to travel throughout the world.

I have been able to research values, sense trends, and make experienced, realistic comparisons. In evaluating an item, it's particularly important to be objective, to separate emotion from intellect.

To begin, here are three essential rules I've developed to simplify the separation of sensuality and sensibility in collecting.

- *Buy perfection.* By this, I mean the item should be in perfect condition. Without a doubt, perfection is the most important element to consider when buying art, antiques, or collectibles. There is no room for emotion here: either the item is in perfect condition or it isn't. This point will be emphasized and reiterated later.

- The item must clearly and distinctly reflect *a specific moment in time.* You should be able to look at the item and get a feeling of where it belongs, its place in history. This is true of all great art, and the greater the piece of art, the stronger this rule is reaffirmed. It is a reflection of the best and most valuable cultural material we relate to. Anything that follows from the work of art is imitative, a repetition or restatement of what went before it. This concept, too, will be further explored in this book.

- A well-ordered collection as an entity is worth more than the sum total of the values of its individual parts. Intelligently selected collections increase in value more rapidly than single objects in direct ratio to the selective knowledge that is applied. Quite simply, one is not as valuable as one hundred. But those one hundred pieces should not be assembled promiscuously. Instead, each item must be chosen for its character, style, and condition. This brings us back to my first rule: condition is the most important element for creating value. Perfection is most desirable.

These rules are the foundation for any sensible and serious buying. Follow them and you're on the right track.

There is a trap, though, and I've seen many people fall into it. The name of the trap is *bargain hunting.* For some reason, when people go out attempting to find a bargain, they leave the rules for sensible buying at home. I believe this occurs because some people hope to get something for nothing.

In the world of antiques and collectibles, you cannot *hunt* for a bargain. Bargains happen when you least expect them. If you think you have a bargain, you must examine the situation carefully.

Most dealers in the collectible, art, or antique business are knowledgeable, experienced professionals. They know their market; a valuable item is not likely to elude them. They set a price relative to the value of the item, its cost, and the necessity of making a decent profit.

If something appears to be a bargain, you must examine the seller's motive. He may be in a situation in which he needs to sell, or, occasionally he may not know the value of what he has. On the other hand, the dealer may be trying to play on your ignorance. The latter is, unfortunately, common enough. A real bargain is very rare.

Bargains do happen, usually when you least expect them.

A number of years ago, on my television show "What's It Worth?" a woman brought in for appraisal a large abstract painting she had purchased at an auction. She bought it because it was big and she liked the colors. It cost her $25. Her first question was whether she had paid too much. I knew immediately that it was worth a great deal more. She mentioned there was another painting at the auction "just like it" which had not found a buyer. Without giving her my reason, I advised her to try to buy the other one from the auctioneer and bring them both to the show as soon as possible. She did, paying $200 for the second one.

Meanwhile I had researched the first painting and when she brought in the second one, my suspicion was confirmed.

Then, on the air, I told her that she had just purchased two exceptionally important paintings by Wassily Kandinsky, one of the originators of the "Blaue Reiter" Abstract-Expressionism Movement in Germany. The paintings were originally part of a set of four, entitled the "Four Seasons," which he did in 1914. Her two paintings, for which she paid $225, I appraised at $25,000 *each.*

The woman screamed with such surprise when I said, "$25,000," that she didn't even hear "each." She was jumping up and down, hugging me, laughing, crying, and screaming in a style that seems common to all winners on television. My program suddenly had all the excitement of a game show when the contestant wins the grand prize hidden behind the curtain.

Today, the four paintings can be seen in New York City. They are exchanged regularly between the Museum of Modern Art and the Guggenheim Museum (which owned the other two). It is important to point out that the four paintings as a group are worth more than the two pairs, and far more than the four separate paintings. In fact, if the set of four were ever sold together, they would be worth over $3,000,000!

This story is an example of that rare exception that proves the rule. Obviously, the seller did not know what he had. But more importantly, the buyer did not hunt for a bargain—it just happened.

EVERYBODY HAS SOMETHING OF VALUE

Had she been bargain hunting, she may have passed over those two paintings.

In my years as an appraiser, I have seen just about everything that people have stored in the attic, personal and historic memorabilia, something someone picked up years ago traveling overseas or purchased at a local garage sale. *Everyone* has one or more objects

Wassily Kandinsky's "Spring," left, purchased for $25, and "Summer," right, purchased for $200, identified by Rothschild as originally part of a set of four Kandinskys painted in 1914, entitled "Four Seasons," appraised by Rothschild in the early 1960's at $25,000 each.

Author examining a painting with infrared and X-Ray.

they are curious about as to authenticity, history and, of course, value. They come to me hoping their paintings, porcelain, teapots, coins, wood carvings or furniture pieces are authentic and valuable.

Over the years, two out of three people who come for appraisals are disappointed when I give them a realistic idea of value. About one in three is satisfied that the item is worth approximately what was paid for it. Only once in about 50 appraisals does the actual value far exceed the owner's expectations.

Each item brought in to me holds some relative value. My objective is to determine that value. In a way, it's not unlike being a detective. I must discover all the "clues" inherent in the object. My investigation frequently begins with viewing the piece under ultra-violet light (to show recent conversions or repairs), examin-

EVERYBODY HAS SOMETHING OF VALUE

ing the item under a magnifying glass or microscope (to study the material more precisely), and occasionally performing a chemical investigation (to determine age, place of origin, and the creative materials of the artist or artisan).

Then I analyze those clues which lead me to conclude the item is either authentic and original or possibly a forgery. Some of my most challenging appraisal problems have been in this area.

I have seen many forgeries or imitations—some good, some bad, some of real value, some not worth the materials of which they're made. There are infinite variations from original work to good copies. Often the copies contain a deliberate or accidental combination of the artist's original elements with atypical additions.

Sometimes the problem can be very tricky. I once received a painting for evaluation. It was a beautifully painted, unsigned portrait of the Madonna. The canvas on which it was painted was authentically of the 17th century. However, the chemical solvent investigation clearly revealed that the paint was recently applied. Therefore, the painting, although it appeared to be the work of an old master, was actually a modern painting in an old style. Since artists frequently copy great works of art as part of their training and occasionally use old canvases to save money, I suspected nothing unusual and appraised the painting at $150.

Later the owner mailed me a certificate indicating the Madonna was painted by a man known as Van Meegeren. I instantly reappraised the work to be worth four to five times my original figure. Van Meegeren was an exceptionally talented artist who had turned criminal. The Madonna was one of his experimental paintings which led to his infamous career as a forger. Interestingly, upon investigating the market on Van Meegeren's works, I learned that his original paintings were bringing in considerably large amounts of money.

This is a splendid example both of what modern laboratory techniques can reveal, and the problems faced by a conscientious appraiser. The possibility of imitation or forgery is just one reason why the serious collector should employ the services of a good appraiser.

Before you even consider buying an item, though, you can prevent an unwise investment by following this preliminary guideline, which will be expanded in a later chapter.

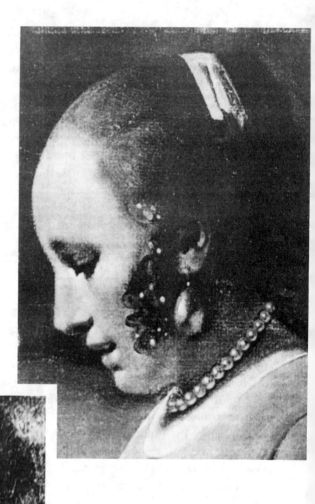

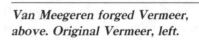

Van Meegeren forged Vermeer, above. Original Vermeer, left.

• Thoroughly study your field of interest. Consider what you
know of the object, its style, and its time of creation.

• Use your eyes to see what is observable about the piece.

• Bring a good magnifying glass (I am never without mine).

• Make sure you examine the object in good light (notice
how many antiques shops are dimly lit—it's not just for at-
mosphere).

• Finally, know its *condition*. I'll repeat this point because
it's that important. Perfect condition is my primary rule of
qualified buying. No matter what the item, prime condition
will ensure continually increasing value.

Value changes constantly. It depends on how many people want
that particular object, whether that style is currently popular,
where it is being sold, how it is exposed for sale, what kind of publicity the sale has had, what similar types and in what quantity are being sold, and all the other factors of the immediate marketplace.

Art Nouveau is an example of a marketing trend. Not 20 years
ago, much of it was considered junk, hideous junk at that. Today,
Art Nouveau objects are some of the biggest investments in the collectibles market. The value of Tiffany glass, due to its inherent
quality and artistry, has gone through the roof.

While not as valuable, Depression glass is another example. Ten
years ago, people were throwing it away (if their parents hadn't already gotten rid of it with post-war prosperity). Now, authentic
Depression glass commands respectable prices and is actively
sought by collectors. In fact, it's so trendy, even imitations are selling well.

Something brand new, whether handmade or mass produced,
seems to go through an immediate period of declining value. For approximately two generations—40 to 50 years—most objects automatically drop in value each year. This is when the item is relegat-
ed to the attic or is thrown out.

Then, after two generations, if the object is still in good condition, it undergoes an increase in value. Whether it's a piece of furni-

ture or a piece of jewelry, if it shows an element of uniqueness or originality, it emerges from obsolescence into what may be a desirable collectible.

This is true of almost any item. Rarely will a new piece increase immediately in value, even if it is of exceptional character, creative artistry, or is made of intrinsically valuable material (such as gold or precious jewels) unless it is purchased as an unusual bargain.

As a rule, anything in good condition that passes through two generations starts increasing in value. A generation can be loosely defined as 20 to 25 years. So today in the 1980's, things that were made in the thirties and forties are beginning to increase in value. Depression glass, as noted, is just one example.

Using this guideline, I predict that in the 1990's many everyday items produced during and immediately after World War II (which are now being discarded) will increase in value.

How does value relate to money? How is a dollar sign assigned to an object? We have already suggested that an object can vary tremendously in value based on its materials, its age, and its creator. Value also varies with demand and quantities available.

So, too, value varies based on the purpose for the specific appraisal. Auction value is not the same as retail value. Value is clear only if its purpose is known and clearly stated. When I am asked to appraise an object, I state its value based on one of 10 categories:

1. Fair market retail value
2. Gift value
3. Insurance value
4. Discount value
5. Auction value
6. Trade value
7. Wholesale value
8. Estate value
9. Distress value
10. The S.R. value method
    (This is a method I created for times when dollar signs block sensible value decisions. You will find more on this in the next chapter.)

Each of these "use concepts" creates a different value for the same object. When you understand the purpose of an appraised value, you gain better control of the buying and selling situation.

Value is an arbitrary thing. Assigning accurate and fair value is an art, perhaps even a science if done by a professional.

In the pages to follow, I hope to share my experience and knowledge with you so that you can use my principles to begin a pleasurable foray into the world of collectibles and antiques, or to enhance your present investment.

You'll learn who an appraiser is, what he does, and how to find a reputable one. You'll gain a professional's understanding of value. You'll discover where to look for antiques and collectibles. I'll share with you seven rules for successful buying. I'll confide my secrets for selling at a profit. You'll find out how to get the most from auctions and how to avoid fakes, forgeries, and other phonies. Finally, you'll have my A to Z guideline for buying anything that has been created on this earth, whether by God or man.

CHAPTER TWO

What Makes
Something Valuable

Some time after my trip to Illinois to appraise that most unusual collection of outhouses I mentioned it during a lecture before a group of antique enthusiasts in Washington, D.C.

After I presented my talk, a man approached me, saying he was with the government. The department he worked for had acquired a tract of land in the coal-mining region of eastern Pennsylvania. On the site of the mine was something unique: a double-decker outhouse! It was to be demolished, but first had to be evaluated.

The assignment was to determine the value of the buildings on the land—and that included this crazy-looking outhouse. As a result of my lecture, he knew I was the man to do the job.

So to the coal mines of Pennsylvania I flew. The outhouse itself was indeed architecturally unique. It's something my client in Illinois would surely have coveted for his collection.

Since the outhouse was not in the best of condition, and consider-

15

ing our more modern concepts of personal hygiene, I gave my appraisal based on condemnation proceeding. Had I given the appraisal for the outhouse collector in Illinois, my dollar figure would have been very different. If the outhouse were part of an estate sale, or was being sold at an auction, or was to be appraised for insurance purposes, the appraised value would be different in each special circumstance.

Value can be infinitely variable. Value is many things to different people. Value is an idea, a concept that is only as accurate as its end purpose is understood.

The double-decker outhouse had no useful purpose at the time to that government agency or to the taxpayers supporting it, and so it was demolished. Now when I am asked to speak, I frequently tell both stories—the first to illustrate my thesis that "Anything made by God or man is collected by someone"; and the second to show how the same object, or type of objects, can have radically different values assigned to it depending on its use. (And it's sometimes said that I have become the country's leading appraiser of outhouses.)

Accurately determining the value of an object is a professional appraiser's work. This is not just fancy guesswork. Instead, there is a fairly precise method applied to fine art and personal property appraisals. Usually, if you compare independent appraisals by competent appraisers, you'll consistently find no wider a variation than about 10%.

The determination of value combines many specific factors, some of which are constantly changing with time and the economic climate. By understanding the rudimentary factors, you can better answer the question, "What makes something valuable?"

To start, any approach to value must include three stages:

Description—Size, color, material, quality, condition, style, age, utility, authenticity, and rarity.

Analysis—Artist's name, the period and place of manufacture, historical association, individual taste, sentimental factors, collection, style, durability, original cost, and the current market.

Evaluation—Retail, gift, insurance, discount, wholesale, auction, estate, distress, and special application or circumstances.

DESCRIPTION

INTRINSIC CHARACTERISTICS AND PROPERTIES

Value is first created by the combination of creative skill and craft techniques with certain materials in a unique manner for decorative purpose or useful function. Since value originates here, let's begin by understanding the 10 general "Description" factors.

Condition

This is the first and most important factor in determining value.

The better the condition of an object, the greater its potential value. An item in perfect condition will command a top price. An item in perfect condition will almost always be more valuable than the same item with flaws. Obviously, there are some objects with minor chips, cracks, or blemishes that sell and even increase in value over time (assuming the condition does not continue to deteriorate). But such an object will never be as valuable as a perfect or nearly perfect piece.

The combination of excellent condition and rarity can be unbeatable. For example, a late 19th century weathervane (not even an official antique yet) in the shape of the Statue of Liberty was sold recently for $82,500. It brought its owner such a remarkable sum in part because the weathervane is the only one of its kind in existence, and also because it survived in the finest condition.

The biggest mistake some buyers and collectors make is ignoring condition. I've seen people pass up a small perfect object in favor of a larger flawed one. I've seen people ruin a perfect object by chiseling away at it or adding on to it in order to "improve" its appearance or function. If you own a Ming Dynasty vase and put a hole through the bottom for electrical wiring to make a lamp, you no longer have a Ming Dynasty vase—you have a lamp.

I always advise my clients to save up for that one really good piece rather than buying several flawed pieces. If you have a collection or part of a collection of flawed pieces, trade them up in order to approach perfection.

Although condition is an essential factor in determining value, condition alone does not set the value when other considerations are lacking.

Several years ago, I looked at a set of 12 chairs in perfect condition that were supposed to have been made in Boston at the turn of the 19th century. A set of this size and age in perfect condition is a most unusual phenomenon. When I examined the chairs under fluorescent lights, I discovered four of them had undergone modern-day repairs and all the rest had been reassembled, recarved, and stained to look old. Unfortunately the chairs, although in excellent condition, were not worth the money paid for them.

The most expensive chair *ever* was auctioned for $275,000. It was an authentic Philadelphia Chippendale side chair, one of 11 or 13 in existence. Just 10 years ago, one such chair sold for just $40,000. Its superior condition earned it over $235,000 in less than a decade.

There are some instances when compromise is necessary or desirable, but to ensure increasing value, aim for perfection in condition.

Authenticity

Authenticity is a major factor in determining value. A reproduction or a forgery cannot be considered in the same light as an authentic piece.

A signature or a date does not necessarily indicate authenticity. A famous name could have been painted on or an "antique" date carved in only yesterday.

To further complicate matters, not all great painters signed or dated all their art works. Rembrandt rarely put his signature on his paintings, although a good number of Rembrandts now bear his name—dealers discovered that adding a "signature" made the art work more salable. The signature does not guarantee authenticity nor increase the value of a work. An unquestionably original painting is equally valuable with or without a signature. Naturally if the painting is a copy or a forgery, the "signature" won't add a nickel to its value. The same applies to dates. (A certificate of authenticity should be a part of every acquisition and appraisal.)

Now, most people can't afford an authentic Rembrandt, a Ming Dynasty vase, or a Louis XIV chair. For this reason, both now and in times past, reproductions are a big business. You can go to any major museum in the country and spend hundreds of dollars on a reproduction. But, even if the reproduction is made from a precious metal such as gold or silver, the item will most likely decrease drastically in value during the owner's lifetime.

Money, or the lack of it, is no reason to compromise on originality. It is better to buy an original hand-crafted piece designed by a local artisan than a museum mass-produced, machine-manufactured reproduction. Better to purchase an oil painting by a little-known artist than spend the same amount on a framed print (which is probably one of thousands) of a famous painting. Owning an original opens the opportunity for an increase in value, a reproduction does not.

Ultimate value to a great extent depends on authenticity. I was once asked to appraise what appeared to be a fine antique American Revolution-style Philadelphia Chippendale side chair. The legs, rails, and backsplat were characteristic of the light, delicate craftmanship of the late 18th century. But on a closer examination of the seat, I observed the tell-tale marks of a circular saw, which wasn't invented until the 19th century. The platform for a seat (the ledge) of an authentic 18th century seat would have had to be hand-chiseled or cut with a straight saw edge. Therefore, I deduced that the lovely chair was a 19th century copy of a chair crafted circa 1775.

An authentic 18th century chair would have been 10 times as valuable as a 19th century centennial commemorative reproduction. The 19th century reproduction was a certified antique, had exquisite workmanship, was relatively rare, and could command a good price, but still was not as valuable as an original.

Age

While age starts from the moment a work is completed, as a general rule, an object's value depreciates for two generations—40 to 50 years. Unless the original market for the object is sustained through an active selling pattern, the first 20 to 25 years of any object's life are marked by declining value. During the second 20 to 25 years, the object has the lowest monetary value. This is often called the "period of obsolescence." However, if the object survives this period in relatively good condition, its value will begin to increase, sometimes dramatically, with each passing year. At approximately 100 years, the object becomes a recognized, legitimate antique. Cer-

Chippendale chairs. Left, early (c. 1760) original, and right, reproduction made for the Philadelphia Centennial, 1875.

tifiable antiques in good condition can command top prices, especially when other value factors coincide.

For example, a combination of age and rarity can cause prices to skyrocket. A silver spoon made during the Middle Ages sold recently for over $24,000 at an auction house in London. This was the highest price ever paid for a spoon. It was considered to have such great value because it was the oldest piece of English silver to come on the market in a long time.

WHAT MAKES SOMETHING VALUABLE?

But age alone does not determine value. There are thousands of coins from ancient Roman times in poor condition still in existence; even though these coins may be well over 2,000 years old, most are hardly worth a dime. On the other hand, an ancient coin found in mint condition, bearing a unique stamp and made from a precious metal, has much greater value.

I use this example to illustrate that no one factor determines value, but rather a combination of factors. This holds true for every object or work of fine art.

Rarity

Regardless of condition or age, rarity alone creates value. Available quantity of any given object has a tendency to reduce value. If a thousand authentic Tiffany lamps suddenly appeared on the market, they would not have the value of the few existing in the market today.

Graphic prints of every style and artistry are popular in today's market. In theory, the artist should print very limited editions, as a small edition creates rarity which in itself means higher value. A large edition usually reduces the ultimate value of any given print. Buyers should make sure the print is numbered and signed by the artist. Without this, the print can only be valued as a decorative item.

Quality

Quality is an important ingredient in determining value. Quality is inherent to the object. It is the intrinsic skill, the underlying ability of the craftsman. While style and taste are highly subjective, quality goes beyond emotional subjectivity and relates to the physical character of the piece itself.

An excellent case in point is an 18th century Louis XVI fall-front desk that was sold in 1982 by Christie's in London for well over $1,000,000. The quality and refinement of its design and workmanship is what brought in the extraordinary price. An art or antique enthusiast must learn to recognize quality, that characteristic element indicating a degree of excellence or superiority.

This recognition of quality can be achieved by reading, and by going to museums, galleries, antique markets, and specialized dealers. Talk to and learn from dealers and sales people. Most of them who are knowledgeable in their field are happy to share information about what gives a piece quality.

Style

Style is the characteristic manner of the artist's or artisan's expression through design. Style is individual to the creator of the object, but is also closely related to the period and culture in which the object was created. Style, in a sense, is a reflection of that moment in time when the object was created.

Identification of style requires knowledge of the elements that are characteristic of style. This can be achieved through education, research, and experience, although not necessarily with a college degree in art history (although this always helps); much can be gleaned from books, museums, galleries, and exhibits. Learning to perceive style is really a matter of recognizing creativity.

Material

Precious or rare materials contribute to the value. Fine porcelain is more valuable than soft paste stoneware; mahogany and other hardwoods are more valuable than plywood; rock crystal is more valuable than glass. (Glass that contains more than 24% lead in its composition is sold as crystal, although it is not—in this case, "crystal" only describes its color.)

But the value in any material lies in the character or quality of the creative skills applied to the object. For example, the great quality of Tiffany glass and other Art Nouveau glass is not so much the value of the material—which is, after all, only glass—but the intrinsic elements of design and a style that reflect a distinct period of time in 20th century art. Essentially, this glass work is a highly crafted art and as such has greatly increasing value.

Color

Generally, color has decorative use as it blends or contrasts in a setting. Selecting subtle or brilliant colors is to some extent a matter of taste, but when considering gems, semi-precious stones, porce-

WHAT MAKES SOMETHING VALUABLE?

Erte sculpture, above, and chair, right, by Edward Colonna, c. 1899, both examples of Art Nouveau.

lain, glass, and even woodwork, there are some specifications for color that relate to value.

Recently I received a telephone call from the west coast about a carved lapis lazuli Fu lion. Lapis lazuli is an azure, opaque semi-precious stone flaked with gold-like particles. The man who had purchased the piece after a business trip to the Orient was anxious to have it appraised, as he had paid several thousand dollars for it.

The moment I saw it, I knew he had paid too much. The color of the stone was too dark and dull. To be of value, lapis lazuli must be rich, deep, and subtle. Furthermore, the carving itself was coarse and garish.

The man had bought it knowing nothing about this stone, but since the piece was large, he was convinced he was getting a "bargain." This is just another example to point out: "if it's sold as a bargain, it's probably not."

Size

Size is important to use, marketability, and value. Very large pieces always present problems. A 10-foot-high cabinet will not fit into a house with an eight-foot ceiling. Two vases that are four feet high are essentially good for funeral parlors. Largescale items are usually only valuable in a museum setting, which is why, in the trade, large pieces are called dogs.

Proportion in size and scale is also important in determining the quality of design, and hence is an element of value.

Utility

Anything that has value also has utility. The item's usefulness may be functional, decorative, or as part of a collection.

A chair is not much of a chair unless you can sit on it. A vase is not useful if it leaks. The utility of a painting is to suit the decor. The use of a postage stamp is as an element of a collection.

One of the first considerations in buying art and antiques is utility. Unless you have use for something, there is very little reason to buy it. If an item is useful and therefore valuable to you, it will probably be valuable to someone else as well.

ANALYSIS

The second phase of determining value is a study of the observable facts relating to the object. "Description" involves the *inherent* factors related to the item. "Analysis" involves *external* factors reflecting personal taste, the current market, and cultural projections.

Artist's Name

The name of an artist contributes to value. However, what is important to understand is that it's not so much the name as the character of the artist's expression and creativity that supports the value of a work, whether it is a painting, pottery, or a piece of furniture.

To a large extent, the value added to an item by the artist's name is really a matter of merchandising or "snob appeal." There are many companies that produce fine china equal to Wedgwood, but somehow the Wedgwood name creates buyer response. (Of course, 19th century Wedgwood has increased in value due to its age, rarity, and artistic character.)

Merchandising or "name" is often the most important asset an object or artwork has. This is generally true of contemporary artists. People frequently buy art not for what they like, but because of a particular artist's name. Sometimes great sums of money are paid for art or objects primarily because of the artist's personality, and his ability to attract media attention and promote himself. The name of a famous artist does not necessarily mean great art. Only time can prove an artist's merit.

But even the works of a recognized master can vary tremendously. I can show you one Rembrandt worth $4.5 million and another only $100,000. The difference is in the quality and condition.

If the object has other value considerations, a famous name adds to its value. If some of these considerations are lacking, a name will not contribute to value.

Collection

An item that is part of a collection has greater value than an individual item. A collection has greater interest and value because of historical, anthropological, social, and/or cultural factors.

Selectivity in collecting becomes a very important element in developing and maintaining value. In other words, quantity does not make value—quality does. I advise my clients to upgrade their collections in quality and condition. This is true of coins, stamps, paperweights, bottles, Civil War memorabilia, 18th century silver toiletry pieces, and anything else.

Cost

The original cost of an object has little effect in determining its immediate or ultimate value. For example, I inherited from my father a collection of speakeasy cards, used as admission passes to speakeasies during Prohibition. These cards didn't cost anything originally—you had to know somebody who was part of the inner circle. Today a card from an unusual club or one signed by Al Capone could be worth $50 or more.

Durability

In household and fine arts appraisal, we have to consider the depreciation of value by use and wear. Lack of durability reduces value. Oil paintings are usually more valuable than water colors, due in part to their durability. Furs, clothing, and personal accessories usually drop greatly in value from original cost.

These less durable objects, however, have a particular kind of value if associated with either historic or social events, such as a costume worn by a movie star, or a flag carried in an important battle.

Historical Association

With proper documentation, historical association can add greatly to value. If you can prove that an object was owned by Czar Nicholas of Russia or Charles II of England or even Elvis Presley, you see sales and value soar.

True historical association can be documented through letters, bills of sale, diaries, photographs, and the like. The buyer should beware of a dealer who claims the object once belonged to George Washington or Benjamin Franklin or John Lennon without evidence or proof. When one buys an object with historical association, the documentation should always be included with the sale item.

In many cases, one must disregard the appeal of association with a famous name. True value is established when the object has historical significance or can be related to the creative or artistic purposes of an artist, inventor, or writer—a letter from Abraham Lincoln showing his inner conflict over the Civil War, or the diary of Claude Monet describing his first forays into Impressionism.

In other words, George Washington's autograph is worth about $300—maybe $500 if it's attached to something like a laundry list. But if it is attached to a document important to the Revolutionary War or to the founding of the United States of America, that could be worth $30,000.

Historical and personal association make for tremendous appeal to the collector, but do not to any great degree add value unless they can be properly documented and have genuine historical or cultural significance.

Market

The market implies the current market, or the popularity and demand for any type of object due to fads, tastes, and trends. Many artists or manufacturing companies are skilled at promotion and sales techniques, creating a demand for their paintings, china, furniture, or bric-a-brac. "Snob appeal" can sustain value for a while, but time alone will adjust this.

I advise my clients to beware of anything that's too trendy. Something that is currently fashionable is almost always overpriced and has a temporarily inflated value that will probably drop in time.

The idea is to buy something *before* it catches on.

During the late 1960's, when fashion leaned toward streamlined, geometric, bold colors and shapes, no one wanted to look at Art Nouveau. Those who bought those delicate, flowing floral pieces paid relatively little for them. Today you can still buy Art Nouveau but at astronomically high prices. (Remember, objects that survive two generations, or 40 to 50 years, almost automatically increase in value.)

There is always a time for bargains, if you can learn to take advantage of a bargain situation. In a depressed economy, if you have the money, this is the time for bargains. At this time fewer people are in the antiques and collectibles market, therefore demand is reduced and prices are lower.

Period of Manufacture

To be particularly valuable, the object must reflect the moment of time—that is, the culture of the period in which it was created. In a way, period of manufacture is related to age, although age itself does not necessarily make something more valuable unless it reflects creative cultural periods. Our culture defines certain periods of time as more valuable than others. We think of great ages in art and style and of historically significant events. Objects that can be proven to have been created during those times have definite value that will only increase with time.

Place of Origin

An object is most valuable at its point of origin. The work of a prestigious New York City silversmith is more valuable in New York than in London. The noted collectors of Haitian art are in Haiti. Eighteenth century American furniture has its highest market in the United States.

An artist or artisan has greater recognition, respect, and appreciation, as well as greater market potential in his own part of the world than anywhere else.

There are a few exceptions, however. When considering masterworks, the market is international. Another exception is the purchase of artifacts from primitive cultures; they must be transported to a more appreciative market. Finally, there are specialized collectors who are not interested in financial gain, but buy purely on aesthetic judgement.

In general, though, professional dealers who buy a piece in other than its point of origin eventually bring it back to that place of origin in order to sell at an increased price. They are following the rule: An object or a work of art is most valuable in its place of origin.

Sentiment

Sentiment itself, while actually a form of love in one of its many varieties, has no monetary value. Therefore it is very difficult to define sentimental value accurately. One man's treasure may be another man's junk. A chipped teapot passed down from your great-great-grandmother may have great sentimental value to you, but because of its condition, could be meaningless to a dealer.

I own a pair of scissors that has great value to me because it belonged to Thomas Edison. The scissors were given to me as a result of an appraisal I did for the Edison Museum in New Jersey, where I learned that they were manufactured by Edison's uncle, who owned a tool-making factory. For me, there is sentimental value mixed with historical value because Thomas Edison handled these shears in his workroom. I will never sell those scissors because no one else would consider them as valuable as I do.

Additional value develops when an individual piece becomes part of a collection. For example, a letter from Lincoln to his wife could be sold at a much higher price to a collector of Lincoln memorabilia than to someone who might want to burn any reminder of Lincoln. (In terms of value, sentiment should not be confused with historical association.)

When buying or selling, sentimental factors do not usually contribute to creating value.

Taste

Taste is merely educated judgement. The development of taste comes from upbringing, experience, education, and personal interest. As a factor in value, taste reflects individual judgement influenced by changing times and customs.

Money does not necessarily create a sense of taste. Essential to the development of taste is a sensitivity to style, quality, and creativity, and an openness to explore, learn, and experience. Taste is the appreciation of the many factors that contribute to value.

EVALUATION

FAIR MARKET RETAIL VALUE

Value is only as good as we understand its use. Fair market value can be described as the price arrived at in a sale in an open market between a willing seller and a willing buyer. (Implicit is the assumption that the buying and selling process is knowledgeable and without coercion or deception.) Retail value takes into account current market factors, arriving at an average acceptable price. Fair market retail value is more hypothetical than actual, based on sound comparables; it is a concept that is needed as a starting point for all accurate value considerations.

Any evaluation must be adjusted to current value. When appraising extremely valuable objects, one must consider long term national or international market trends, which are cause for more detailed examination.

In general terms, let us consider 100% as the average fair market retail value for the purpose of understanding the many other kinds of value.

Gift Value

This is the monetary value placed on an object to be donated to an institution, museum, or charitable organization. This type of appraisal is necessary to claim a tax deduction for a gift contribution.

Gift value (in law, stated as Fair Market Value) is a high legitimate value, regardless of its original cost. Gift value can be 10% to 25% higher than fair market retail value.

While gift value is generally treated as being on the high side, if the price is too far removed from an actual fair market retail value, the Internal Revenue Service may challenge that value.

Conversely, there are instances when a low gift value may be more advantageous to the donor, such as when personal property is given out of generosity to an individual (usually a relative or future heir). Tax laws post a monetary ceiling on the amount that can be given at one time before incurring gift tax.

One of the largest gems I've had to appraise was a rough, uncut sapphire that was tentatively to be donated to the Smithsonian Institution in Washington, D.C. The full crystal was about the size of my forearm. The stone had partially destroyed an oil well piping in the Persian Gulf where it was recovered. We studied the crystal and saw that possibly 36 really good, beautiful gems could be cut from it.

Had the owner offered the sapphire for sale, he could have sold it for $750,000 to $850,000, but would have had to pay a tax on the

14 pound uncut sapphire, one of
the largest gems ever appraised by
Rothschild.

potential capital gain. In giving the stone, which I appraised at $1 million, he would have saved a great deal of money with a tax-saving gift deduction. He died, however, before any transaction was made, and his wife claimed the sapphire as personal jewelry. I couldn't imagine where or how she could wear it—it weighed 14½ pounds.

Insurance Value

Insurance value should be accurately projected slightly higher than normal retail value, based on the concept of protecting the client and theoretically replacing the lost, damaged, or stolen item with another piece of comparable kind, condition, and quality. Certainly in an inflationary marketplace, this is justified. I usually consider insurance value to be 20% higher than an immediate market cost.

One must consider depreciation due to wear, exposure, and changing styles. Many items decline in value for two generations, or 40 to 50 years. Conversely, one must also consider the fact that current replacement cost may be many times higher than original cost, due to uniqueness of style, designer name, rarity, quality of the object, and intrinsic value of the material.

The client, the appraiser, and the insurance company should be made aware of these possible variations when determining an insurance value.

Discount Value

This is also referred to as cash discount dealer value, or a trade courtesy. A good dealer will frequently discount retail price by 10% or 20% for a preferred customer or for a cash sale. Discount value, therefore, is about 80% to 90% of fair market retail value. Slightly lower than this is a jobber, runner, or agent's discount.

Auction Value

Auction value is generally lower than fair market retail value. This is caused by a dynamic conflict between buyer and seller, and sometimes at least two competing buyers. The auctioneer is obviously motivated to achieve the highest possible price and the buyer is motivated to obtain the article at the lowest possible price. Because of this battle, the actual selling price has a tendency to vary greatly.

There are always special exceptions, for example: a husband and wife bidding against each other, or an auctioneer who is holding to a reserve price (the minimum acceptable offer), whatever the reason, and will not sell or accept bids below the reserve at auction.

A lower selling price is created by a variety of factors: poor sale location, wrong timing, inclement weather conditions, conflicting dates, unattractive cataloguing, inadequate promotion, improper presentation, even an auctioneer with a dull personality.

Conversely, factors that make for a higher than usual auction price are a skillful, informed, forceful auctioneer, attractive display, proper promotion, careful cataloguing and effective advertising. Others are association, rarity, publicity, sentiment, and speculation.

Trade Value

The practice of trading, swapping, or bartering seems to be increasing. Trade values frequently average 65% of fair market retail value.

When bartering with a professional dealer or a private party, get some cash and you may wind up ahead. Dollars balance out any barter situation to the benefit of at least one trader—a technique that's essential for making a satisfactory deal.

Wholesale Value

Wholesale value is theoretically 35% to 45% of fair market retail value. This is due to quantity purchased at a low original cost, low transportation cost or overhead, and/or quantity available at time of sale. Overstock, reduced demand, and imperfections directly reduce the value of materials to be sold.

It is generally not possible for the average buyer to obtain an item at wholesale, but as the saying goes, "It pays to have an uncle in the business."

Estate Value

According to the law, estate evaluation must be stated as fair market retail value, but realistically in larger estates this can be as little as ⅓ of full value. Professional appraisers try to protect the interests of the estate, but there are many facets created by lawyers and the individual requirements involved which tend to produce lower values.

Estate sales occur as the result of a breakup of a home, death, or personal financial problems. The sellers or heirs are usually under stress and are rushed into a sale. In addition to emotional factors, there are sales commissions as well as legal and administrative costs which obviously reduce the net return of the property being sold.

In some cases, sale at a reduced price is a financial necessity. A few years ago, I appraised an amazingly perfect 15-carat, deep-colored emerald that I considered at the time to have a fair market value of a quarter of a million dollars. The owner was slightly disappointed because he had just paid $265,000 for this stone. Unfortunately, the owner died a few months after he purchased this beautiful gem. If the fair market retail value had been used as the estate value, the other assets of the estate would have been forced into liquidation in order to just cover taxes. This would have created a financial disaster for the heirs. To prevent a needless forced liquidation of major property, the estate tax commissioner and I arrived at a compromise value of $85,000 for the emerald. After the appraisal and tax settlement, the heirs sold the emerald to a dealer for $185,000. The gem was purchased not long after that by a European dealer for close to $300,000.

Distress Value

A "forced sale" price can be as low as 10% of fair market retail value. This occurs when the seller must sell due to ill health or economic pressure. The forces that so dramatically lower a selling price include personal hardship, liquidation pressure, or relocation.

S.R. Value Method

While one cannot appraise sentiment, a special kind of value occurs in an emotionally-charged situation such as divorce or dispute over inheritance where personal property is to be divided rather than sold.

I use a technique to determine value by giving items a numerical value from one to 100, using no dollar values whatsoever. By removing the dollar sign, one creates a more comfortable situation for selectively dividing the property. This permits the opposing parties to better recognize other elements of value such as personal taste and needs, and therefore make more personally satisfying decisions.

To sum up, all appraisal problems can be considered to have three basic components, which become the requirements of any accurate appraisal.

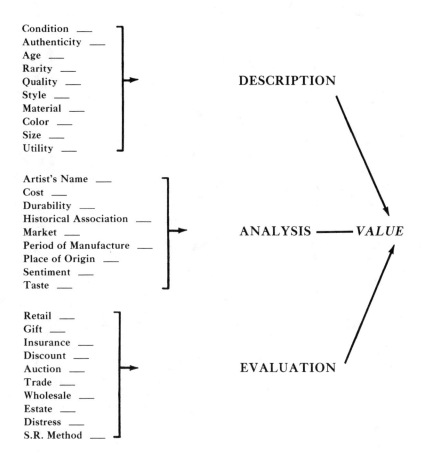

Condition ___
Authenticity ___
Age ___
Rarity ___
Quality ___   DESCRIPTION
Style ___
Material ___
Color ___
Size ___
Utility ___

Artist's Name ___
Cost ___
Durability ___
Historical Association ___
Market ___   ANALYSIS ——— *VALUE*
Period of Manufacture ___
Place of Origin ___
Sentiment ___
Taste ___

Retail ___
Gift ___
Insurance ___
Discount ___
Auction ___   EVALUATION
Trade ___
Wholesale ___
Estate ___
Distress ___
S.R. Method ___

It must be understood that the factors presented here under three broad categories are only an introduction, the broad brush strokes, of the work done by a professional appraiser. Remember, there are infinite variations to consider within each category to consider such as constantly changing tastes, condition of the object in question, and local markets, which can and do affect ultimate market value. There is no substitute for experience and knowledge.

Anything created by man out of natural materials, skillfully and artistically modified, has a definite intrinsic measured value, once there is knowledge of the dynamic factors that make up value.

CHAPTER THREE

All About Appraising

In the past 40 years, I have appraised everything from Javarro Indian material to an Egyptian mummified bird, many fine paintings and collections, gems, silver, books and libraries, memorabilia, coins and stamps, furniture, and a variety of other personal property.

I thought I'd had just about every challenge an appraiser could experience—until one afternoon when I received a phone call to appraise for insurance purposes a herd of elephants.

The method of appraising elephants is the same as with all other forms of appraising: determine value and find basic comparables.

Since my personal knowledge of elephants was limited to which end was front and which end to avoid, I needed to make a few telephone calls to obtain the precise information regarding the cost of a live, healthy elephant of specific age, weight, and sex. Further exploration of this evaluation problem took into consideration transportation, maintenance, care, shelter, feeding, and veterinary costs. These attested factors allowed for a precise evaluation.

Appraisal is a statement of an accurate, realistic, and observable value that requires basic knowledge of known comparables and the specific use of any given value. Appraisal is *not* the art of educated guessing.

The process of appraising is truly interdisciplinary, requiring both general and specialized knowledge. The appraiser must be trained and equipped to research the individual value problem by various techniques. He should be skilled in scientific techniques of examination, including x-ray and fluoroscopy, infrared photography, ultraviolet examination, chemical and physical analysis, and micro and macrophotographic comparisons. The consideration of an individual value problem might include the use of market research, reference literature, study collections, and museums. An appraiser should also have a network of specialists as well as knowledgeable dealers and collectors as professional resources. In addition, the appraiser should be well versed in many disciplines, including sociology, history, religion, economics, geography, and anthropology, as well as be knowledgeable in art history, and have the ability to recognize creative expression as it relates to time and place.

Due to my years of experience, I can identify a certain object, such as a Chinese vase, simply by looking at it, sensing its weight, and feeling the textural quality. What appears to be an instinctive reaction (or guess) has its foundation in experience, knowledge, and observation.

But there are times when I honestly don't recognize the precise value of an object. I have stood in front of an audience of thousands of people and said in response to a question concerning the value of a particular object: "I don't know." This has earned me more authority and credibility than bluffing would have.

With time and research, however, one can uncover the facts and information needed to assess value. I've sent my staff out for days to do the research enabling me to write an accurate appraisal.

Who should consider the services of a professional appraiser? You don't have to be the owner of a herd of elephants or a wealthy collector of art, antiques, or jewels. Everyone has something of value. Anyone who has valuables at home—silver, gold, precious jewelry, paintings and other valuable artwork, Oriental rugs, fur coats, fine antique furniture, collections (whether stamps, coins, or comic books), and any inherited valuables—would do well to have an expert appraisal confirming their value.

Items are appraised for a number of reasons, including authentication, curiosity, personal satisfaction, gift and estate tax determination, liquidation and investment. Much of my work today involves estate or gift tax determination and insurance coverage.

Homeowner's insurance policies set very low limits on jewelry and silver, and may not have any direct provisions at all for antiques, artwork, and other collectibles unless the items in question are specifically covered in the contract.

Without proper appraisal, which will permit special insurance to be purchased, a homeowner has little protection from loss, damage, or theft of valuable possessions.

Unfortunately, too many people think they have coverage or believe their policy does not require appraisal. If your home had been burglarized and $5,000 worth of your jewelry was stolen, but your policy had a $500 limit, you would have lost $4,500.

Many people call an appraiser after a loss, trying to get a value based on a description, but insurance companies rarely accept such ex post facto appraisals.

You should keep inventories, sales slips, or photographs of your valuables. These are proof that you did indeed own a silver tea set or a Queen Anne side chair, although only a valid appraisal can determine their dollar value. This is what an insurance company will need to know before paying you.

Inflation or a changing market can also influence an insurance payment. For example, a painting bought five years ago for $2,000 may now be worth $10,000. Unless there has been current appraisal, the insurance company would only pay $2,000 if the painting is stolen or destroyed.

Therefore in order to protect yourself, you should have your possessions reappraised regularly and buy adequate insurance to cover them. When these two critieria are met, there is almost never a loss with insurance collection. (Since the cost of insurance premiums can vary greatly due to numerous factors, it may be beneficial to shop around for the best policy.)

On the other hand, you do not want to overpay your insurance premiums if there is a drop in prices. For example, a large, relatively perfect diamond had a retail purchase price of $60,000 in 1980. Not even two years later, the diamond's value price plummeted to around $30,000. Silver is another example of changing values; it was worth over $40 an ounce for a time, but has recently dropped dramatically. If you purchased a diamond ring or a set of sterling silver flatware and had it appraised at your purchase price, your insurance premiums are now too high. Furthermore, if you suffer a loss, your insurance company may not necessarily pay you at the original retail value. If your silver tea set for which you paid $5,000 can be replaced at $3,000, that's all the insurance company may be required to give you.

An accurate, competent appraisal will also help you when dealing with the Internal Revenue Service. I have seen many taxpayers lose most of their claimed charitable or gift deductions because of faulty or improper appraisal preparations. If the IRS, for whatever reason, negates an appraisal, you may be involved in lengthy and costly litigation.

Some of the most frequent questions I hear are: "Where can I find a good appraiser?" What should a complete appraisal include? and "How much will it cost?" These are difficult questions, since so far no state laws exist regulating, certifying, or licensing the nation's estimated 125,000 men and women who act as fine art or personal property appraisers. Anyone can buy a gold lettered APPRAISER sign and declare himself in business.

There is no formal educational program for appraisers, nor is a qualified appraiser required to belong to an appraiser society. However, membership in one or more of the major appraiser organizations does imply a certain degree of experience, ability, and knowledge needed to prepare accurate value statements.

One way to find an appraiser is through a recommendation from a banker (particularly one in the bank's trust or estate department), a lawyer, or even a friend or associate who has had a thorough, satisfactory appraisal. Occasionally, a local museum or gallery can offer a recommendation. If you need an appraisal for insurance or estate purposes, it's a good idea to use an appraiser approved by your insurance broker or banker.

You can also ask for a recommendation from an appraiser society. Some of the most prominent societies are the American Society of Appraisers, The Appraisers' Association of America, and The International Society for Fine Arts Appraisers. Members of these organizations must have at least five years' experience and are tested for competence.

When gems are considered for evaluation, a certificate from the American Gemological Society will guarantee that the appraiser has passed a rigorous technical course in diamonds and colored stones. But this does not mean his expertise necessarily extends to gold or other precious metals. (There is a need for this type of control established by the jewelry industry in the profession of arts and antiques appraisals.)

Most appraisers are listed in the yellow pages and are generally affiliated with local auction houses, galleries, or antiques shops. I do not recommend using a dealer as an appraiser because of the potential for conflict of interest. Some dealers may over-appraise the value of an item they want to sell you in order to gain a higher price, and may under-appraise your object in question in order to buy it at a low price. The same applies to appraisers affiliated with auction houses—there is simply too much room for misrepresentation on a number of levels. For the same reason, never have anything appraised by a department store.

There are many knowledgeable, ethical dealers, however, who act as appraisers and separate their appraisal work from their dealing practice. Once they appraise, they don't buy. As a matter of ethics, an appraisal should remain entirely separate from any buying or selling relationship because this situation reflects a direct conflict of interest.

To recognize a good appraiser, I recommend using the following guidelines:

1. Ask the prospective appraiser if he is qualified to make your specific appraisal. In other words, a generalist may be best for most objects, but may be unable to accurately appraise jewelry, coins, stamps, or antique books.

2. Question the appraiser about his qualifications. Don't be afraid to ask questions concerning the appraiser's training, education, and professional experience. Find out if he belongs to a major appraiser's organization and verify that information. Ask for references and follow up on them.

3. The purpose of the appraisal—insurance, gift, wholesale, es-

tate, etc.—must be discussed. For tax purposes, the appraiser must state the use and standard definition of fair market retail value.

4. The appraiser should not have or have had financial interest in the object to be appraised. This is particularly important in any tax situation.

5. The appraiser should show a willingness to call on or recommend an outside authority if the particular object lies beyond his range of expertise.

A formal appraisal should include several key elements. Never accept an appraisal or a bill of sale that would say, for example, "One antique table. $500."

The following should be included in any written appraisal:

A detailed description of the item—size, age, significant markings, material, artist's name, historical association, rarity, and every other factor relevant to value.

The object's provenance—its history, why or when the work was commissioned, who owned it throughout the years, and proof of authenticity. (Appraisal should not be confused with authentication. Proving an object's authenticity may require a considerable amount of work and is charged separately.)

Manner of acquisition, date of purchase, and statement of original cost—particularly if the item was purchased within the last ten years.

A quality color photograph of the object—frequently a good, sharp photograph testifies more precisely than words to the character and quality of the appraised subject.

A statement of comparables upon which the appraisal was based—such as sales of other objects of similar quality and kind, quoted prices in dealer's catalogues, the current economic state of the market, exhibitions or displays, and (in artwork) the artist's standing in his profession. The appraisal report should state the sources for this data.

The date of the appraisal—at the time of its commission.

The appraiser's signature—not a corporate name or stamp.

Insurance, estate, or tax evaluation reports should include the appraiser's qualifications and resume. Keep a copy of the appraisal for yourself before mailing the original to your insurance company or the IRS.

How much can you expect to pay for the services of a professional appraiser?

Fees vary widely according to the location, the individual, and the object in question. In most cases, appraisers charge by the hour or by the day. The range of hourly rates is $50 to $150. Daily rates commonly range from $300 to $1,000. Travel costs and expenses are extra. Jewelry appraisers charge anywhere from $10 to $100 and up.

It's a good idea to ask your appraiser what he charges and ask him to estimate the number of hours needed to complete the job before you authorize a formal appraisal. Fixed fees on extremely valuable items can often be negotiated.

Frequently, it is less costly to bring the object to the appraiser, rather than have him come to you. Some auction houses and galleries offer reduced prices if the item is brought in. This is certainly advisable when there is little or no risk in moving the material to be appraised. Of course, this is not always possible—large, heavy, or fragile pieces usually require the appraiser to travel to the object.

Stay away from appraisers who charge a percentage of the appraised value. This practice gives the appraiser leverage to over-appraise an item in order to increase his fee. You may be in for an unpleasant surprise when the IRS questions the value, or in the case of its loss, you discover you cannot collect from your insurance company.

It is important to recognize the distinction between the appraiser and the critic. The appraiser must use critical judgement, but this judgement must be objective and realistic. Personal bias and subjectivity should not enter into an evaluation. To accurately judge value, the appraiser must be completely objective, and impersonal, and the appraisal opinion formed without prejudice or ulterior motive.

How often should you have your valuables appraised? Because of inflation and constant fluctuation in the marketplace, I generally advise my clients to have a reassessment about every three years. Extremely valuable objects may need to be appraised more frequently. Artwork, in particular, can rise or fall in value dramatically within a short period. Similarly, if there is a rapid drop in certain markets, such as diamonds or precious metals, it is wise to get an updated appraisal.

Appraisers should charge much lower rates for properly inventoried items that have been previously appraised. The major part of the valuation having already been completed, the appraiser may need only to know the current market.

Value is a constantly changing phenomenon. Sometimes an appraisal can be valid for over a decade. Other times, a year may see a drastic rise or fall in value. Changing tastes, revived trends in style, and recently recorded comparable sales modify the value of objects treasured or considered trash in the past. The appraiser's job is to relate these variables to reflect the market today.

CHAPTER FOUR

Where to Look for Antiques and Collectibles

Many years ago, I took a leisurely day trip through upper New York state and came home with a collection of very fine antique guns and other firearms. They turned out to be quite valuable, but I didn't pay a penny for them. In fact, I discovered them thrown out at a roadside dump!

Valuable material can be found everywhere—from junkyards to basements to attics, from flea markets to estate sales to auction houses. Great values can also be found at garage sales, thrift shops, hobby meetings, and even dump sites, as my experience will attest. The fun and excitement of discovery is always possible. Searching for art, antiques, and collectibles can be endlessly absorbing. Don't limit yourself to established antique shops, shows, and auctions.

Of course, the idea that treasures can be found on trash collection day is not new. My grandfather used to bring home great antiques he found in the refuse heaps at "better" addresses. A fortune can be made just picking up stuff that's been thrown out before the garbage trucks get there. People frequently cast away what they consider clutter without realizing these objects could have real value if dusted, cleaned, and repaired. Of course one must learn to pass by the junk, but the reward comes in transforming one person's trash into your treasure.

When you look for objects of value, I firmly recommend an open mind and an observant eye. You may be surprised at how much material of potential value is out there.

Most people are not aware that they probably have in their possession something that warrants further study and valuation. Many people don't realize the value or the marketability of the objects they own. They may be curious, but simple inertia keeps them from actively discovering value.

You can begin a treasure hunt in your own home. Re-examine everything you own in the light of your own values and the value guidelines set forth in this book. Sort through the material you have stored away in boxes, bureau drawers, cabinets, closets, shelves, desks, even your car trunk. Search your attic, kitchen, den, garage, and basement.

Resist the temptation to throw out objects more than 25 years old. Remember, most objects go through a period of declining value for approximately two generations. If the item is maintained in relatively good condition, it then starts rising in value. At this point, the object will often become much more valuable and certainly will be worth more than its original cost.

During the past 30 years, I have been happy to tell innumerable clients that their grandparent's hand-me-downs or heirlooms had more than sentimental value. Consider every object you own as having potential value. Maintaining any object in fine condition is an investment for the future.

Collectibles are frequently found at thrift shops and charity outlets. These organizations are often run by people who aren't aware of the value of their inventory. This opens up bargain possibilities. If you have a sharp eye, a thrift shop can be the perfect place to discover objects of value. Of course, one must sort out the junk from that which may have potential value. Again, I emphasize that condition is important. Choose only those items in relatively good shape.

Garage, yard, tag, or house sales are popular and offer another opportunity to find bargains in antiques and collectibles. Garage sales are usually run by homeowners trying to get rid of objects no longer wanted or needed. Sellers in these circumstances are usually willing or are forced to sell cheaply.

Flea markets have become a leading source for undiscovered valuables. Don't assume they only sell junk or that the "good stuff" can only be found in fine antique shops. Not so. The term "flea market" has become a generic expression for antique fairs, groups of small antique shops located under one roof, as well as outdoor open markets selling antiques, "quasi-antiques," used household goods, clothing, old souvenirs, and the like. With any degree of perseverance, you can find objects that have very good value because the dealers, in many cases, may not know all they need to know about their merchandise. This, of course, can create a pleasurable situation for the buyer.

Street fairs, outdoors shows, or antique shows are still other places to uncover valuable antiques and collectibles. One often has to see through the piles of over-priced material, but now and then one can find objects that are quite good and can be bought at bargain prices.

Several years ago, I held an appraisal clinic at an outdoor antique show in Bridgeport, Connecticut. Toward the end of the day, a man presented me a tarnished silver three-piece tea service for which he paid $400. Upon examination, it was easy to determine that it originated in New York City circa 1730 and, once polished, it was worth conservatively $6,000—certainly a prize discovery.

On the other hand, I was shown a silver teapot with a rather ornate coat-of-arms, purchased for $300. Upon close examination, the teapot turned out to be only silver-plated and the coat-of-arms was readily identifiable as having descended from the Ritz-Carlton Hotel in Boston. I don't think the teapot could have commanded more than $30, even if the hotel wanted it back.

I will admit that dealers at antique shows have first crack at the merchandise. Frequently, they trade and buy among themselves before opening hour when the public is admitted. This practice is often the most rewarding result of showing their wares.

The public can still strike good deals, however. Keep your eyes open for booths that are closing before the show is over. This indi-

Silver teapot, c. 1730, part of a tea set purchased by owner for $400, and appraised by author as worth $6,000.

cates poor sales, and the dealer may be more receptive to discounting his prices. In general, the time to ask for a lower price is just before the closing bell.

Antique shops are obvious and traditional places to find collectibles. Generally, I advise those who visit chic antique stores in cities or even country shops, to be prepared to spend a lot of money. The top dealers offer prestige and often the best pieces. These are professionals who know their merchandise and market. They always give a detailed bill of sale and, in general, conduct business to maintain their status and reputation.

These factors, plus expensive overhead and high real estate taxes are reflected in the prices, making it almost impossible for the average buyer to uncover a bargain. Therefore, I suggest you start haunting suburban and country antique shops. The best situation is one in which there is a concentration of shops grouped in one geographic area, whether a town or a street. This allows for healthy sales competition. Comparison shopping is definitely recommended whenever possible.

Auctions are another traditional outlet for buying and selling antiques and collectibles. In my opinion, the major antiques houses are becoming less important to the average buyer in terms of discovering bargains. While the occasional bargain may arise, the extensive publicity surrounding these auctions creates heightened desire and demand—and prices rise accordingly.

Ordinary, local auctions that are not heavily publicized offer much better opportunities for realistic buying and bargain possibilities. Local auction houses often have objects that might be great treasures. For example, I have seen many more fine American paintings sold at small, provincial sales than have passed through the major auction houses.

One can find listings for upcoming art and antiques shows in national antiques and collectibles magazines, in antique dealers publications, and in local newspapers and publications, where times and places of auctions are frequently advertised. One can also find listings in "penny-saver" and "bargain shopper" newspapers published in most communities across the country. Every local newspaper also announces nearby flea markets, fairs, church raffles, etc.

Yet another source for finding antiques and collectibles is various trading, hobby, or collector's clubs that exist for specialized areas and materials. Information about them can frequently be found in publications specializing in that particular area of interest.

One last word: I don't recommend buying antiques or collectibles through the mail. Most reputable dealers don't want to risk putting their fine materials in the mail; it's not a sensible practice. Furthermore, the buyer doesn't really know what he's purchased until he's paid for it and received it. A photograph and a description in a catalogue just isn't a substitute for actually seeing, handling, and examining the object in person. The only exception might be when dealing with a reputable seller who offers the item on approval with a full refund if it is found unacceptable for whatever reason.

Once you are in a buying situation, how do you select that one good piece? I've had many clients say to me, "I'm not very good at picking out the winning horse..." or "The stocks I choose always lose money..." or "I never have any luck in the lottery... so how am I going to find something valuable in antiques?"

To find "gold in the old," your best approach is to become something of an expert in a specialized area—whether Civil War memorabilia, rock 'n roll miscellany, late 18th century English porcelain, or Art Deco automobile hood ornaments.

How should you choose an area of interest? Let your instincts be your guide. Select a specialty that is personally intriguing. Choose something you like, that you find appealing for whatever reason.

Many people shy away from staking out a specialty because they lack confidence or experience, or any number of external factors. ("My friends will think collecting World War II comic books is silly.")

Ideally, the choice of subject matter should be understood in its own terms and enjoyable for itself. If you choose a subject because you think it will impress your friends, or because it's currently in vogue, or even because it happens to be selling right now, you will deny yourself the profound pleasure that collecting should be. Ultimately, the only purpose for buying any type of object is to enjoy it, regardless of monetary value.

Yet another advantage to specializing is the fact that a collection is worth more than the sum of its parts. As I stated in Chapter One, this is one of my essential rules for buying. Unrelated individual items are not as valuable as a carefully assembled collection of items.

Unfortunately, people often buy objects at random, without taking the time or thought to build a collection. When you go antique hunting with nothing particular in mind, just hoping for "a good find," you actually reduce your chances of buying an object of value. The sheer volume and vast selection of items on the marketplace can be overwhelming, making it almost impossible to focus on that which might bring you pleasure and, hopefully, profit.

Moreover, most people do not have the broad foundation of knowledge extending over many areas to discriminate between choices. On the other hand, if you are knowledgeable about one specific area, you will be better able to judge whether the object is worth the price and whether it will increase in value.

Thus I strongly advise anyone with an interest in art or antiques to specialize. By specializing, it is possible to pick up a good deal of knowledge in a given field in a relatively short amount of time. This knowledge can be acquired by reading books on the specialized area of antiques or the specific period in which you are interested. Libraries and many bookstores have at least some material on your chosen interest. Some even have entire sections on antiques and collectibles where you can locate a number of books written specifically about Chippendale furniture, Japanese art, French crystal, antique dolls, baseball cards, etc. As a general rule, current books on a given subject are better than older publications.

To augment your knowledge, visit shops that have the type of items you're interested in buying. Ask questions. Most dealers are. very pleased to explain the finer points of quality, style, and value to a potential customer.

Compare prices. Find out how much other items of the same period are worth. Write down this information on a note pad and begin a reference file.

By studying the material or the period of interest, you can gain a tremendous advantage in acquiring objects of value that can be subsequently sold at a profit.

When buying, bear in mind a corollary worth repeating: Buy the best you can afford. It's better to buy one good item than several lower-priced, lower-quality pieces. In other words, if you have $1,000 to spend, buy that one excellently-designed object in superior condition rather than ten $100 pieces. Experience has shown that higher-priced items tend to appreciate in value more rapidly than cheaper items.

I also advise anyone in a buying mood to equip himself with the proper tools: a good magnifying glass (at least a 6-power and preferably a 10-power) and a flashlight. Use your eyes and the magnifying glass to learn the facts of the material you are considering. Use the flashlight to illuminate the object, to examine crevices or corners, and to see things you would not see under existing lighting conditions. In my opinion, the magnifying glass and the flashlight are the most important tools for the collector and antiques sleuth to find identifying marks and to spot flaws. Moreover, by coming equipped with these tools, you are signaling the dealer that you are not an uninformed amateur.

In addition, I suggest having on hand a tape measure to size furniture, decorative objects, and paintings. I hate to tell you how many times I've had someone come to me saying that he bought a beautiful credenza but it's four inches too long to fit the space he has available. There's very little to do but sell it, often at a loss. If your dealer has a kind heart, he may take it back for a credit. I also suggest having on hand room measurements and dimensions of walls, floor space, etc., so you won't miss a good buy because you don't know if it will fit your space.

To recap the basic guidelines for successful antique sleuthing:

- Art is where you find it, and it can be found everywhere. Great values can be discovered from local flea markets to international auction houses.

- Be persistent. It may take some time and effort to find that special object worth owning.

- Become an expert. Research and familiarize yourself with quality and costs of an area or period that interests you.

- Buy for pleasure. Spend your money on what *you* like and will enjoy having.

- Build a collection. A collection is always more valuable than individual pieces.

- Strive for perfection. Avoid cracks, blemishes, and flaws. Damaged merchandise will never increase in value as much as perfect or near-perfect objects.

- Have the right equipment with you—a good magnifying glass, a flashlight, and a measuring tape.

If you come across an unexpected discovery or have purchased something of real value, I advise you to learn more about it. Check reference books or catalogues. See a specialist who has a collection or the experience with which to compare it. Take the object to a professional appraiser to determine authenticity and monetary value.

It is very important to care for your purchase. Dust it off, polish it, keep it clean, and maintain it in good condition. Treat it as a potential treasure whether it is or not. If you love it, it's a treasure.

Above all, keep an open mind. Remember, good buys on art, antiques, and collectibles can be found just about anywhere. Talk to other people. Keep your eyes open. Take a few chances. With no risk, there can be no gain. Use your imagination to project an object's worth once it's cleaned or repaired.

With that kind of enthusiasm, some degree of persistence in pursuing the marketplace, and a little bit of luck, you may find that elusive, unexpected bargain and have an enjoyable adventure along the way.

CHAPTER FIVE

Seven Rules for Successful Buying

In the 40 years I've been in the business of appraising art and antiques, I only once found a genuine bargain. It happened a number of years ago. I purchased from a major auction house a bronze Buddha figure for $85. It was a nice piece about 14 inches high with a little green stone, which I presumed to be glass, on its forehead. I did not imagine I had a bargain, but purchased the statue because it pleased me.

I took the statue home and cleaned it carefully. After buffing the stone, it seemed to me rather bright in color. At first I thought the color of the glass had been enhanced by foil in the back, a common technique to increase the vibrancy of refracted light.

To satisfy my curiosity, I scooped the glass out and examined it. To my great surprise, it turned out to be a large, well-proportioned, exceptionally brilliant emerald!

I then sold the emerald for $3,000! Afterwards, I found a piece of green glass, replaced it in the Buddha's forehead, dusted it with cig-

Bronze Buddha, originally purchased by Rothschild for $85, with "glass" stone in forehead which turned out to be a genuine emerald that Rothschild removed and sold for $3,000.

arette ash to "antique" it, and resold the figure for what I had originally paid—$85.

So in this one instance, I actually discovered a bargain and made
some money. Now, if I were to buy every bronze Buddha with an
unidentified stone in its forehead, I would certainly never again
happen on such a bargain—and would probably end up with my
original Buddha with the green glass.

That's the reality of buying antiques and collectibles. If you learn
nothing else from this book, I'd like to leave you with one very fundamental rule: Don't shop for bargains.

Bargains simply happen and usually when you least expect them.
If you purposely look for bargains, you'll rarely find them and a lot
of money will be wasted in the process. Beware of any dealer who
offers you something as a bargain—it probably isn't. A low price is
often a tip-off that something is wrong. If you go around buying
"bargains," you'll generally get secondary quality questionable in
taste. My experience as an appraiser has shown this time and time
again: Bargain hunting is the worst thing people can do.

However, bargains do happen. Occasionally the seller may not
know the true worth of his merchandise. This is a bargain opportunity if you are in the position of being educated in a particular subject or area to recognize something of value at a bargain price. If an
article is being sold by an obviously less informed person than yourself, then by all means buy it if you can afford it. Take a chance!

Other times, the seller may have to lower prices because he is under duress—he can't pay his taxes or the rent is due and he hasn't
had a sale all week.

Then there are certain sale conditions, such as a country auction
on a rainy day where there aren't too many people. You might just
find that bargain piece of furniture or painting. Again, you have to
buy with prior knowledge or experience and have some recognition
of quality and style.

I would advise against anybody's buying anything *just* because
it's a bargain. Let me stress again that bargains are unexpected. In
fact, they happen so rarely I'm willing to take the position that a
bargain *never* happens when you look for it. It happens accidental-
ly, the fortuitous coincidence of time and place.

Once you have this concept firmly in mind, the actual rules for
successful buying are surprisingly accessible and simple, in spite of

the fact that many people believe they are complex secrets carefully guarded by those who manage to buy consistently well.

Over the decades, I have distilled the countless "tips" and "guidelines" down to seven essential rules. The amount of money you have, or don't have, is not a factor. In every case, these rules apply whether you are spending $25 or $25,000.

Accordingly, in order of importance, my seven rules for successful buying:

1. BUY WHAT YOU LIKE

The first general rule for successful buying is to buy what you like and will enjoy owning. Since bargains can prove so serendipitous, the average person should buy for pleasure, for use either functionally or decoratively, or to complement a collection according to the scale and size of his needs. But that doesn't mean what you buy for pleasure won't be worth more later. When you're interested in buying, find something that appeals to you personally, even if it is not a bargain, and even if you have to pay top price for it. Spend enough to capture that particular piece. Don't let something of true value slip away because you don't consider it a "bargain." If the object holds strong individual interest, it will probably be of value to other collectors and dealers and therefore will increase in monetary value should you decide to sell in the future.

Above all, it is most important that *you* like the object, otherwise you're throwing away your money. Along these lines, don't buy anything *just* because it's discounted—it's not a bargain if you can't live with it. Before opening your wallet, ask yourself, "Do I like it?" and "Will I be able to use and enjoy it?" If you find something you like, buy it for the pleasure it gives you, not because you think the item is trendy or because you hope to make a profit reselling.

Don't confuse "pleasure value" with "investment value." In particular, avoid any material that is offered promotionally as having automatically increased value in a relatively short time. Examples include collector's plates, ceramic figurines, silver offerings, and similar kitsch. These are advertised as exclusive limited editions increasing in value "X" percent per year with a potential resale market of "millions" of collectors. In reality these "limited" editions run in the tens of thousands, *decrease* in value each year, and have a resale market that is actually meager.

One example is a series of silver ingots, each etched with the image of one of the Presidents of the United States, selling for about $29.50 apiece. However impressively packaged in a presentation box, the encased silver ingots have only a meltdown value due to their large minting and to the lack of artistic character in the etchings.

These and other such items may give the owner pleasure through sentimental association or because they're "cute," but any item that is factory made and mass produced has little lasting monetary value. If you like an item for the pleasure it gives you, buy it. Just be aware that this is precisely the purpose for which you are buying and not for resale investment.

Again, to clarify my first rule, don't be afraid to spend money for something you like. When it all boils down, the only valid reason to buy art, antiques, and collectibles is for the pleasure it gives you. Keep your purchases in good condition and they will continue to give you pleasure. The "pleasure motivation" should be the primary motivation for successful buying.

2. BUY PERFECTION

By "perfection" I mean the state of preservation and original condition. Poor condition reduces value. Merchandise with cracks, blemishes, or damage has only limited possibility for increased value.

A very fine Lowestoft bowl—late 18th century porcelain—with an age crack in it will begin to bother the collector more and more. It will never be as salable as a perfect piece. Only objects in perfect condition continue to maintain or increase in value.

Certainly your purchase should be kept in good condition or even improved, but in general, restoration has a negative effect on value. I would like to believe that most dealers would tell you if an item has been restored, but that's not always the case. I've seen sets of furniture that were sold as being in perfect original condition. However, when the chairs were examined under ultraviolet light, I'd find that three out of four legs, for example, had been replaced or restored.

You have to learn to use your eyes and depend on your own resources. You can't blindly trust in the dealer—he could show a piece and attempt to hide any damage. This is true whether you're buying porcelain or paintings, furniture or decorative objects.

I suggest buyers carefully examine an item before purchasing. Take along your magnifying glass and flashlight. You might even wish to invest in a portable, battery-powered ultraviolet light. This tool will show you flaws and repairs that can't be seen with the naked eye.

Look for perfection and don't be embarrassed to do so; you can't be too careful. However, use your imagination. Often an item may be only dusty or grimy and tarnished. If you can examine the item through the dirt to determine if there are any flaws, a good cleaning or polishing may be all that is needed to restore the piece to perfect condition. But be realistic about repairs. Don't buy something that needs resurfacing, soldering, rewiring, or carpentry. Major repairs and restorations may not only be costly if you can't do them yourself, but they also reduce value. When something is in very bad condition, don't buy it.

On the other hand, if you need six dining room chairs or a bedroom dresser, and restoring or repairing the item will make it functional, it is perfectly all right to buy—but do not consider your purchase from an investment standpoint.

3. LOOK FOR RARITY

Rarity is one of the most important elements of value. Quantity generally reduces value. I once was interviewed by Joe Franklin, the radio and TV personality. He mentioned that he had a large collection of 78-RPM records. Well, they will never be valuable—even though the musicians are long gone and the *music* is great—because the discs were produced in such large quantities. Moreover, many of them have been re-recorded on slower speeds, producing a better quality of sound. After all, people generally collect records for the *music*, not for the joy of owning pressed plastic.

By the same token, a print by a great artist in editions of 10, 20, or 30 is much more valuable than the same image that's printed by the hundreds.

This rule applies to art, furniture, porcelain, or any item. True rarity equals a potential increase in value.

But extreme rarity or uniqueness does not necessarily make a piece valuable. Shrunken heads are not very valuable. Most of them are fakes—they're monkey skins that have been dried over a rock. But even the real thing won't be valued at much greater than $100. Once I received a shrunken head with a kind of grey, leathery-skinned scalp. It turned out this was the result of a Navajo rite performed on a white missionary. I valued this at $500 because of its relative rarity. But in general, it becomes very difficult to evaluate this sort of object except as a curio.

However rare an object is, it must be collected by other people in order to gain value. I stand on my original premise that anything made by man or God is collected by someone. The law of supply and demand dictates that the greater number of people collecting or desiring to collect a limited supply of a certain item or type of items, the greater the monetary ratio:

$$\frac{RARITY}{DEMAND} = VALUE$$

4. THE ARTIST'S NAME COUNTS

The name of the artist, artisan, craftsman, designer, or manufacturer is one of the essential elements of successful buying. This holds true for paintings, furniture, porcelain, crystal, or whatever.

By identifying the artist, we can locate the object according to place and time, two other important factors that add to value. We associate great names with creativity, craftmanship, and quality of design and execution. A great name lays the groundwork for great value.

For example, take the furniture produced in the late 18th century by Townsend Goddard of Newport, Rhode Island. In that area, imitations made by craftsmen who worked for Goddard are collected and sold. But these men didn't have quite the touch of the master; one can look at the different pieces and detect differences in style and quality. The work of a master is almost always superior to pieces made by lesser artisans.

If you are knowledgeable about material, you can place precisely—in terms of quality and price—an accurate assessment of value.

Conversely, one must beware of "names" that have established fame (or notoriety) merely through publicity. As I've mentioned previously, some artists living today earn high prices for their canvases primarily through the reputation they've gained in the gossip columns and the cocktail party circuit. Owning their "creations" may seem chic today, but the works will probably lose quite a bit of value in the future.

From an investment standpoint, don't buy something simply to impress others. To emphasize this point, I'd like to reiterate my first rule of buying: Buy what *you* like, not what you're supposed to like.

The "media manipulators" notwithstanding, I can't stress enough the importance of the designer's name in placing the piece within a time frame and craftmanship inherent to the work. A great name creates the dynamics for successful buying.

5. ASCERTAIN AUTHENTICITY

Always obtain proof of authenticity. Authenticity is a high measure for value. Imitations or reproductions may be the sincerest form of flattery, but they will never have the value of an original. In order to buy successfully, it is extremely important to obtain proof of authenticity.

If you are knowledgeable, you can authenticate a piece on your own. It helps to have the correct tools. Most purchase mistakes I have seen occur when buying a piece that had been tampered with. For example, I see a lot of antique porcelain on which the maker's mark has either been added by overglazing, or in some cases, has been scraped off and covered with a varnish. This is usually easily detected under ultraviolet light.

Deliberate misrepresentations by sellers happen infrequently. I still believe most dealers sell as honestly as they can. However, some are less knowledgeable than they ought to be and some are just naive. Everyone can make a mistake, even I.

Years ago, I bought at auction a pair of cuff links that were reputedly worn by Abraham Lincoln. It turned out in investigation that the cuff links were of Japanese origin and were owned by Mr. Lincoln's son. Now that's obviously not the same as if they had been owned by the President. As I said, nobody's infallible. You take a chance and it's part of the fun of buying.

Although the majority of dealers are honest, one cannot be too careful. Even a certificate of authenticity might not be authentic. One notorious faker of paintings used to furnish phoney certificates of authenticity for an extra $50. Years ago there was quite a business in selling forged certificates.

If you are spending any great deal of money, you should obtain some sort of authentication or legal verification from an appraiser or a specialist.

In order to obtain professional authentication, you will have to be able to take the item to the appraiser or specialist. Reputable dealers with whom you have a buying relationship will often let you take the item for study for 10 or 20 days. I've known clients who have kept a piece for six months until they could obtain adequate authentication.

Of course, the buyer must leave a deposit for the item, sometimes the full amount. Make sure you have a written understanding that a full refund is guaranteed if the piece is found unacceptable for any reason.

Ideally, you would have enough time to carefully consider or study the piece before buying. But sometimes you have to rush to buy a piece, as when somebody else is competing for it. I support the premise that occasionally you have to take a chance. Go with your intuition.

6. GET A DETAILED BILL OF SALE

Along with proof of authenticity, it is essential that the buyer receive an itemized bill of sale. Don't accept a receipt that says: "One antique desk—$1,000." There is too much room for misrepresentation. In the event there is something seriously wrong with the piece, you would have little legal recourse. A detailed account will help assure your legal rights should there be a dispute about the object.

I had a case some time ago concerning an early 18th century porcelain urn that was sold as "slightly repaired" for $14,000. My client asked me to examine it. Those "slight repairs" turned out to be 14 major structural defects. This was a gross misstatement of value. My client went to court, I testified on his behalf, and he won back his money plus the cost of litigation.

The bill of sale should specify style, period, date of manufacture, and designer's name (if known), dimensions, material, provenance, and the sales history of the piece. If the dealer or seller has any additional knowledge about your purchase, this too should be included in your bill of sale.

A reputable dealer will not hesitate to write out a complete bill of sale. If a seller refuses your request for an itemized bill, you can be certain he is not really selling what he claims to be selling.

In general, do business only with well-established, reputable dealers. Avoid sellers who come into town with a flock of paintings or items, rent a selling space for three weeks, and then disappear. If you can't find the seller, you will be unable to get your money back should the item prove to be phoney or valueless.

One must be particularly cautious when buying in a foreign country. Just recently I was looking at a collection of nine pre-Columbian terracotta pieces from Peru. My client had purchased them from a young Peruvian boy whose father brought them down from the mountains. Unfortunately, those two natives were skilled in making very thorough fakes; the pieces were too zealously polished. They were decorative and would make nice flower pots, but they weren't the valuable collector's items for which the buyer hoped.

This happens in Peru and it happens in Paris—it occurs throughout the world, including this country. Although this does not occur as frequently as one might expect, I do see this kind of thing often enough.

Such errors in authenticity can be avoided through education. The greater your knowledge of a particular type of object, the less risky your purchase. Learn about the material you're interested in—the difference between good and bad, top quality and poor quality, authentic and fake. Learn to recognize the specific clues that indicate a particular style or period.

Terra cotta Columbian-style figurine that is an elaborate fake, broken and repaired. Fluorescent examination illustrates the obvious.

7. LEARN TO RECOGNIZE QUALITY

For the serious collector, there is no substitute for thorough study of the specific field of interest. Before buying, gain some knowledge of the type of object with consideration of the various elements that constitute value. Research and familiarize yourself with what denotes quality within the item or period that interests you.

Learn the time periods of style. Develop an ability to identify the work of particular artists or artisans. Learn to recognize originality in line and form as it reflects that moment in time when it was created.

Above all, learn to recognize quality.

What are the elements that make for the best or the highest quality? Obviously, each specialized area of collecting has specific requirements that require study. However, there are some universal guidelines that can help the buyer to recognize quality.

Of primary importance is the quality of *simplicity*. Look for simplicity of line and simplicity of statement. Regardless of which period the piece originates from, the design should not be muddled or confused.

There should be a sense of *unity*. The design must move and flow around a single element. The piece has to be orderly; the texture and color must be unified with the design.

The piece in question must be *complete* both in concept and in the final product. It should not have been cut down from a larger size or reassembled from two or more separate pieces.

The item must have a certain kind of *expressiveness*. It must have something to say. Admittedly, this can be an individual subjective reaction.

Look for *variety* in the piece, or a variation of a theme. For example, there are four legs on a chair. Two legs are identical but they're facing in opposite directions. This is more unique than four legs all pointing in one direction as in modern functional pieces.

An object should have a pleasant *texture*. Coarse or rough material may make for an interesting design, but it doesn't have the same quality as soft or smooth material. Most people don't realize the importance of sensory reaction. The desire to touch or to handle a pleasing texture is part of our human nature and therefore is considered an element of value.

Some items can have an inherent *complexity* which contributes to visual interest. This is related to the skill of the artist. The nature of the complexity may be profound or subtle, it may even be funny, but it should not be confused or contradictory.

Color is a most important factor of quality. The appeal of certain colors is highly personal and, of course, the colors must blend into the desired environment. You wouldn't put a green painting over a purple couch (although I've seen this done). In general, brighter colors have greater marketability than dull, monotonous colors. The buyer must also be able to recognize the manner in which color is applied. I look at many paintings and find them amateurish because the painter doesn't know how to blend or use the colors skillfully enough to express his ideas.

The buyer must also be able to identify the trivial—pieces commercially made in large quantities without skill or artistry. One almost has to be able to define poor quality before one can really appreciate high quality.

In essence, look for an overall *aesthetic* quality that appeals to you. Learn to recognize line, form, and proportion. In terms of decorative material, it must function in its designated setting. It must be well constructed, soundly built, and in good condition. Be sensitive to color and texture. Finally, look for simplicity, unified design, and variety within that design.

To summarize, my seven rules for successful buying:

1. Buy what pleases you.

2. Buy the best condition possible.

3. Look for rarity.

4. Choose recognized artists or manufacturers.

5. Make sure you buy originals.

6. Get a detailed bill of sale.

7. Learn the craft of collecting—become knowledgeable in the recognition of quality.

And most importantly: Never shop for bargains.

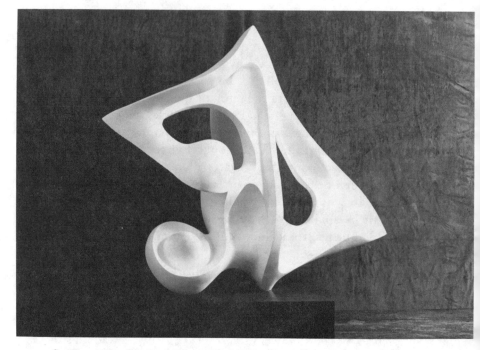

Sculpture by Rothschild entitled "Wind and Rain," illustrating form, line and proportion.

Let us say you have found that perfect antique that fits all of the above criteria and you have the money to pay for it. Should you negotiate the price?

In some cultures, particularly in Europe, Mexico, and the Middle East, bargaining is expected. In fact, you'd probably insult the seller if you simply paid the first asking price.

In this country, however, the question of bargaining is touchy. Many Americans feel uncomfortable about "haggling." As a matter of decorum, I would discourage "bargaining" over only a few dollars. It's demeaning to the seller and makes the buyer seem cheap.

However when substantial savings are at stake, I would say bargaining is generally acceptable. It never hurts to offer. The worst that can happen is that a dealer who is high-hat might react rudely and throw you out of the shop.

But bargaining need not be ill-mannered. There are ways to reach a middle ground resulting in a satisfying transaction for both buyer and seller. I've seen it done skillfully and even charmingly a number of times.

To overcome initial hesitation about bargaining, it helps to realize that few price tags are firm. Most dealers are flexible in their prices. Some dealers even inflate their asking price because they expect some degree of negotiation. For example, it is extremely common for a dealer to automatically lower the price by 10% when offered cash.

One way to approach the delicate art of negotiation is to tell the dealer you like the item, then ask whether he would consider taking "X" amount of dollars for it. Be reasonable—don't ask to buy a $100 item for $10. Generally, 10% to 40% less than the original price is fair. Do the arithmetic in your head and then state a dollar figure; dollars sound much better to dealers than percentages. Of course it always helps to mention that you'll be paying in cash.

Never disparage the merchandise, hoping that because you find it inferior, the dealer will sell it to you cheaply ("You've got to be kidding to ask so much for this piece of junk!"). Also, avoid setting yourself up as an authority when you're not ("This couldn't possibly be an authentic Lalique crystal vase!"). Merchants take pride in their goods and most know their material. Insulting, rude, or pushy behavior is no way to strike a good deal.

On the other hand, dents, chipped paint, and other signs of disrepair should be politely pointed out. If the piece has not already been discounted because of flaws, you can probably buy it for less.

Unless you fear the item will be snatched up by another buyer, make time your ally. If you can't get the price you want, come back later in the day when the dealer may be more amenable to lowering the price if the item still hasn't sold.

When shopping at an antiques store, return the following week. If the item remains unsold, the merchant may then accept your offer. I have known clients who would go back to an antiques store every week for months until finally the seller acquiesced.

Bargaining is something of a game. Neither side wants to lose face—or money. If the negotiation process is handled courteously, the dealer most likely will not be offended and you will probably wind up with a successful buy.

Before concluding, I'd like to offer some basic tips for the novice:

- It is not necessarily true that the more things cost, the better they are.

- An item need not be an antique (over 100 years old) to be valuable.

- Don't be taken in by the label "antique." Most items sold in antique shops are not certified antiques. Beware of any seller who refers to his merchandise as antiques unless he can prove it with appropriate documentation.

- Comparison shop if you are in the market for a particular item. A set of six Queen Anne style mahogany chairs tagged at $3,000 at one antique shop may be purchased for only $2,000 at a shop down the street. A Royal Doulton figurine may be auctioned for $25 at an estate sale, but may be priced at only $10 at a church fund-raising bazaar. It's a good idea to check out as much of the market as possible to find the best buy on the item you want.

- The best time to look for antiques and collectibles is at off-times, when most other people are not shopping. For example, buy late in the day when a dealer may be anxious to make another sale before closing. Shop on rainy days; there is nothing like bad weather to keep people away from antiques stores, auctions, flea markets, etc. If possible, do your hunting mid-week; weekend crowds encourage dealers to hold out for higher prices.

- Don't gamble foolishly. Don't spend your life savings on something about which you have little knowledge.

- If you absolutely must have that necklace, painting, silver tray, or whatever, and you can live with the price, buy it when you see it. It may be gone if you wait too long.

- Study each item for its individual merit—don't assume that because the dealer is selling genuine Mucha posters that the Art Nouveau jewelry is also authentic.

- Don't automatically pass by items, booths, or shops that don't seem very popular. You might just find the buy of the year.

- Don't be taken in by fast-talking or aggressive sellers. Remember, buy what *you* like, not what the dealer wants you to like.

- Don't be in a hurry to buy. Consider all the value factors as outlined in Chapter Two. Most importantly, keep in mind condition, color, and creative expression.

- Think about the utility of the item. How will you use the object? Will it fit in the place you have in mind? If you're buying for investment, get enough professional information about its future market appeal.

- The last rule I can give you is to handle the item carefully and make sure it is well protected on its trip home.

If you stick to the rules that have been suggested in this chapter, you're going to come out ahead and be on your way to a lifetime of successful buying.

CHAPTER SIX

Selling for a Profit

My father, who was an antique dealer, could sell a beggar a safe to keep his money in. My dad used to say that the proper way to make a good profit was to mark up an item ten percent. Only he figured that a ten percent profit came from buying for one dollar and selling for ten.

Some people have visions of converting their collectibles into cash. Stories abound of the silver teapot, handed down from a great aunt, fetching thousands of dollars at auction. Or the painting picked up at a flea market which turned out to be a long lost masterpiece and sold to a private collector for a quarter-million.

Tremendous profit rarely happens and, like a bargain, it happens when you least expect it—it is usually a matter of luck. When the amateur goes looking for profits on his purchases, he frequently ends up red-faced instead. Although there are many enticing books available promising that you can "get rich selling antiques and collectibles," it is unrealistic to expect a phenomenal profit. But it is quite possible to make a measurable profit.

There is a growing market for art, antiques, jewelry, rare books, rugs, furniture, and a vast assortment of memorabilia and collectibles. Most people would obviously rather not sell their valuables at garage sales or flea markets, yet they come to realize that their possessions aren't quite in the class of the few major international auction houses. Still, there are avenues for successfully selling almost anything if you understand the rules of the game.

The average person who wishes to sell for whatever reason would do well to become familiar with the individual or company to whom he is selling. Unless you are selling to a friend, chances are you'll be dealing with a professional.

To stay in business and make a reasonable profit, the professional dealer must double his money;there must be a 100% markup, called a "keystone" markup. (A double keystone is always a very happy event.) Therefore, a dealer will have to sell your item for about twice what he is paying you. (If he can't, he's better off in another business.)

Let us say you have an 18th century Chippendale chair made in Philadelphia with an appraised fair market retail value of $2,500. This is the price the dealer can expect should he try to sell the chair. At best you would receive $1,250 to $1,500, from the dealer on the sale. The dealer would then try to sell the chair at keystone or perhaps a little more—in other words, at fair market price.

The average owner of an antique or collectible will rarely be able to get the full appraised value when attempting to sell. A more realistic expectation is 35 to 80% of appraised fair market value. This may come as a great disappointment if you were anticipating making a fortune on the sale. Separating fact from fantasy, however, will prevent you from making costly mistakes in buying or selling in the near future.

Now, this does not mean the dealer is running away with a 100% profit off of your investment. He must deduct overhead, salaries, taxes, insurance, and slow periods with no substantial sales. I've seen many failures in the antique business because the dealers didn't take these factors into account.

There have been occasions when I have been called in to examine the economic structure of a small antique business. The dealer would show me an item he bought for $10 which he tagged to sell for $12.50 and I knew that if a customer was really interested in buying, the dealer might even sell it for $11 with the idea of making a new customer or a better profit on the next sale. There are troubled times when a dealer may have to sell at a loss just to pay the rent. This is a distress situation which can occur (and may turn out to be the time for a bargain). From the dealer's standpoint, it's better to take a loss and survive.

To sell for a profit, it is essential to determine what your item is worth as well as your basic costs before you even begin.

The first step is to obtain a professional appraisal, especially for valuable antiques, collectibles, and jewelry. You still may not be able to sell for the full appraised value, but a proper appraisal will at least let you know what the item is worth in today's market and what you can reasonably expect to ask as a starting price.

Occasionally, I have encountered a client who wants something appraised very high to make the item seem more valuable to sell. But I, and most other ethical appraisers, will generally set an appraisal only as high as fair market retail value will allow.

To find an appraiser who can estimate the market value of your material, check the yellow pages of your local telephone directory or contact a major appraiser's organization, such as the American Society of Appraisers or the Appraisers' Association of America. Collectors' groups or antique shop owners can also suggest names of authorities or specialists. A few auction houses and some art dealers provide free appraisals if the item is brought to them.

Second, you have to calculate your gross expenditure. How much did the item originally cost you? Did you put any money into it to have it cleaned, repaired, or restored? Will it be necessary to advertise the sale, and how much will it cost? Are there any commissions to be paid to an agent or the auctioneer?

Third, one must take into account the general economy, including inflationary trends.

Let us say inflation in one year was 10%. If you bought an item in January for $100 and sold it in December for $110, you have not made a profit. Obviously, since many objects are kept for years before they are sold, long-term inflation must be calculated.

On the average, you can expect good material to increase in value only 5% to 10% per year. Therefore, from an investment standpoint, most antiques and collectibles are poor profit-makers, especially in light of continuous inflation. For this fundamental reason,

I say to the average art and antique enthusiast: If you're buying as a hedge against inflation, you're in the wrong boat. There are better and safer ways to shelter your money.

This past decade provides a telling example. Double-digit inflation produced a storm of buying as the average person spent ever-escalating sums of money on art, antiques, and collectibles in an attempt to stay financially afloat. This unprecedented demand for collectibles, however, washed in a tide of mediocrity. When inflation subsided, the demand abated and buyers were left with a residue of low-quality collectibles.

This phenomenon of frantic buying at swollen prices is cyclical. When it is over, people invest instead in tax shelters, stocks, bonds, and money market funds.

There is nothing surprising about this. These trends follow a law of economics that should be learned by anyone who is in the market to buy for resale purposes. *When the inflation rate is higher than interest rates, the market for art, antiques, and collectables rises. Conversely, when inflation rates are lower than interest rates, this market drops.*

There is and will always be one important exception to this rule. The top of the art market will continue to thrive regardless of the economic and political climate. I interpret the top of the market to include the old masters—the great works of artists such as Cezanne and Picasso—and the finest examples of furniture, jewelry, and "objets d'art" of any period. These not only hold their value against inflation, but indeed set new price records.

High quality and perfection always make for sound investments. Medium quality, mediocre design, and faddish items are speculative investments at best.

Does this mean that if your walls are not hung with Rembrandts and your furniture is not authentic Louis XV, you should forget about selling in today's market?

Not at all.

The demand for unusual collectibles is greater than one might expect. There certainly is a market for very good to excellent quality merchandise. Items are constantly circulating and recirculating. People sell for various reasons, usually due to changing lifestyles, a move to another residence, the need to raise cash, a death in the family, or just a change in tastes.

SELLING FOR A PROFIT

Desirable collectibles have the potential to increase in value from 20% to 30% a year. The best occasionally can gain anywhere from 50% to several hundred percent within a year's time.

A good example of rapidly growing value are lithographic posters by Alphonse Mucha. An original poster featuring Sarah Bernhardt

Alphonse Mucha (1860 - 1939) poster which sold for under $500 ten years ago, but is worth $5,000 today.

which sold for under $500 about 10 years ago is now selling for around $5,000. And five years from now you could probably sell it for over $10,000.

Another unusual collectible is a set of Elvis Presley bubble gum cards from the mid-1960's. Five years ago, a collector might have picked the set up for $100. Today, it's selling for around $300. I figure five years from now it will go for $600 to a specialized collector of Presley memorabilia.

A few examples typical of the collecting categories increasing in value are listed below. The prices in the list are fair market retail value and are drawn from actual sales or appraisals.

All of the following prices are assuming fine or excellent condition, one of the most important factors of value.

Object	Late 70s	Early 80s	Late 80s (estimated)
Civil War binoculars	$ 20	$ 50	$ 125
Martha Washington doll made by Parian & Bisque	$ 200	$ 325	$ 550
Coca-Cola tray (about 1910)	$ 35	$ 175	$ 400
Edison Gramaphone (about 1915)	$ 350	$ 550	$ 900
Bronze Indian figure by Remington (about 1905)	$ 2,000	$ 3,800	$ 8,500
Slant top desk, mahogany, Philadelphia (about 1795)	$ 5,000	$15,000	$30,000
Valentine card (about 1900)	$ 10	$ 30	$ 65
Walnut highboy, Massachusettes (about 1760)	$15,000	$20,000	$45,000
Art Nouveau brass andirons (about 1900)	$ 200	$ 375	$ 850
Mason pattern fruit jar	$ 25	$ 40	$ 75
Elephant folio hand-colored lithograph of Audubon's original watercolor.	$ 850	$ 1,850	$ 4,500
Baccarat paperweight, French (1848)	$ 700	$ 1,500	$ 2,500
Sanderson silver tankard, Boston (about 1675)	$12,000	$20,000	$30,000

Your best bets for further information about your specific subject of interest can be found in specialty books, museums, collectors' groups, and knowledgeable, cooperative dealers.

SELLING FOR A PROFIT

Valentine, c. 1900, left, and Walnut Highboy, mid-18th Century, below.

Baccarat Paperweight, left.
Sanderson silver tankard, below.

Another method to increase your potential financial return is to simply hold onto your collectible long enough until you can sell it for a good profit. The reason for this is two-fold: Once an item is over 40 to 50 years old, there seems to be a natural increase in value. And, as the years go by, chances are good that comparable items will become scarce.

Now, hanging on to your collectibles until they become rare antiques may not be your idea of excitement, but many people tell me that if they had not been in such a rush to sell they might be enjoying a happy profit today.

For example, in 1965, I made the mistake of selling my large collection of speakeasy admission cards for $1,000. One of the most important cards was personally signed by mobster Al Capone. Today, because of the mushrooming market for unusual collectibles, that card alone would go for $1,000 and the collection as a whole for $5,000 to $7,500. According to my calculations, the collection should more than double in price over the next five years because of its rarity and because it reflects a unique moment in history.

Considering that the speakeasy cards were a gift from my father, you could say I made a profit. But I lost out in a dramatic way—on potential profit.

It is one thing to contemplate potential profit—an appraiser says your item is worth "X" number of dollars—and quite another thing to achieve the net dollars. An actual sale has to take place before you can declare anything as a profit.

Currently I am acting as an agent for a wealthy couple on several fine paintings being offered for sale. One is a Picasso they purchased last year from a very well known gallery at $300,000. They want to sell the painting for $400,000. After researching the market, I informed the couple that I can sell it for $325,000 to $330,000, but not $400,000.

They preferred to hold onto the painting until they could get their asking price. The couple owns $25 million worth of art, so they are in no danger of starving; they can afford to wait.

If you are in the market to sell, how can you place a reasonable price on your merchandise?

Recognizing the market certainly is the essence of good professional practice. You can't escape the current economic facts of life: You have to know the marketplace. The more knowledgeable you are in your field of particular interest, the better position you will be in to turn a profit. You can determine the present market value of an item by researching recent pricing guides available in most bookstores, as well as talking with dealers and collectors groups.

You can get a good idea of how much other people are willing to pay for comparable merchandise by investigating antiques shops, flea markets, auctions, and estate sales. Also check newspapers and

Examples of speakeasy cards, c. 1920, above, and facing page.
Courtesy of The New York Historical Society, New York City.

antique trade publications. Accurate pricing must be based on sufficient data. Your original purchasing price is not usually a good indicator of present values. The item might have been worth $10 when you bought it, but it isn't necessarily worth $10 when you're ready to sell it.

If your material has been appraised, this will also give you a general dollar figure to work from.

But I think one of the best ways to determine a reasonable price is to simply put yourself in the potential buyer's shoes. How much would *you* pay for the item? *Objectively* examine your item for what it is. There is no monetary value you can put on love or senti-

SELLING FOR A PROFIT

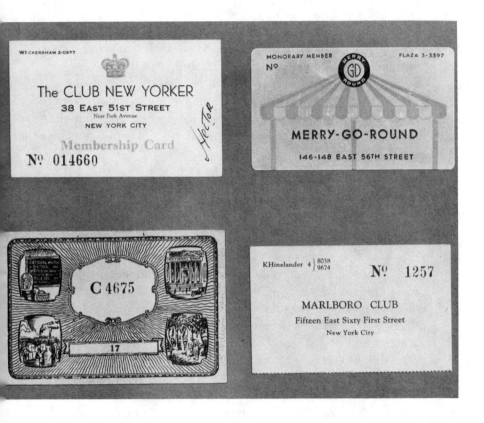

ment. Your grandmother's tea set may be priceless to you, but is just another tea set to a potential buyer.

On the other hand, I think that for resale purposes, one should certainly consider re-examining any associated or historical relationship that can have a measurable bearing on immediate value.

If your grandmother's tea set was used when she entertained Helen Hayes as a young actress and you have an old photograph of them sipping Darjeeling together, you have just added value. Tell a potential buyer the item's history, if you know it. Being able to say that the tea set was brought over from Russia when your grandmother escaped during the Revolution may increase its value to a potential buyer (assuming the set is not stamped "Dishwasher Safe—Made in Japan").

Know your merchandise. If at all possible, research the name of the artist or manufacturer. Where was the item made? Of what material and quality is it made? What style is it in? The more information a potential buyer has, the more he sees value; therefore, he is more inclined to buy at a higher price and you are more likely to make a profitable sale.

If you're buying with the intention of investment, look for perfection. Condition is so important when you're buying, and even more important when you're selling. Many times I've heard a potential buyer say, "Oh, I love that," but when they see a flaw, they back out of the sale. It is particularly difficult to sell a less-than-perfect item to professional dealers.

Having built my career in the repair and restoration business, I am acutely aware of how essential good condition is. Several years ago, I saw a collection of over 4,000 doll house miniatures valued at $375,000. This particular collection contained the largest assortment of miniatures that it has been my pleasure to see. For me, the greatest pleasure in viewing this collection was its prime condition, which in itself would ensure its continually increasing value and salability. As a seller, you must be aware of what condition represents in terms of aesthetics and how much any violation to perfection will cost you in terms of profit.

There may be the temptation to cover up an imperfection or to fail to inform a potential buyer of factors you know would reduce value. One should never misrepresent the reality of what one is selling. The unhappy consequences of deliberate misrepresentation may be a law suit after the sale.

Now, one of the rules of value that is frequently forgotten by the seller is that a pair of objects is worth more than the items sold separately. A pair of anything is worth one third more than the total value of two single items. If one item was worth $500, a pair would be valued at $1,333. (This rule does not apply to commercial, mass-produced products.)

A collection is also always worth more than the sum total of individual items sold separately. Just recently, a 403-piece set of old Tiffany silverware sold for $39,000, which averaged out to almost $100 per piece. This is far more than one could get for a single fork or one place setting. This Tiffany collection had 18 place settings; its completeness added dramatically to the sales value.

One exceptional item belonging to a collection is much more valuable than the same item by itself. To whoever now owns my speakeasy cards, the Al Capone card is worth more if kept as part of the set than if sold as an individual item. If you are selling to make a profit, sell the whole collection as a package; don't sell only the "star" of your collection even if you think you can replace it.

Once you have set a price, leave a little room for bargaining. In any sales situation, you should be prepared to allow a discount, especially if offered cash, if your profit is assured, or if one person is intent on buying a large number of items.

When you have an idea what your item is worth and have estimated a realistic price, you will want to know *where* you can get the best selling price.

The person who decides to sell has six major outlets:

1. Private collectors

2. Art or antiques dealers

3. Antique shows

4. Collectors' organizations or clubs

5. Local or national auction houses

6. Advertising in local media or specialized publications

If you decide to go to a dealer, it pays to offer your item to a specialist. Don't give the 18th century Italian violin you inherited from your uncle to a local shop—you'll receive much more money from a specialized dealer of antique musical instruments. If you have a painting to sell, find a knowledgeable dealer specializing in the particular subject matter, whether it is 19th century English landscape artists, Impressionists, 20th century abstracts, etchings, or posters.

You can find a specialist by asking at an art gallery or antiques shop, or by contacting one of the national appraisal societies.

Be prepared to negotiate with the buyer. It helps to be armed with a professional appraiser's estimate of what your item is worth. Remember, though, that your appraisal is based on fair market retail value, which is the price at which the dealer can expect to sell your item. You will probably receive considerably less.

Beware of dealers who offer to appraise your collectibles with the intention of buying it—there is an unquestionable conflict of interest represented here.

If you are not satisfied with the dealer's best offer, he may agree to take the item on consignment for a selling price upon which you both agree. The dealer will then charge you a 10% to 25% commission on the gross selling price.

You may do better by selling on consignment because the dealer can take the time to wait for the right buyer. But in most circumstances, I generally don't recommend letting your items out on consignment. An object consigned to a dealer allows for consistent misrepresentation. Simply put, a consignment dealer may take your $100 item and three months later call you up and say, "Well, the highest bid I got was $40." The dealer may not have worked hard enough to sell your item, or perhaps has not held onto it long enough for a buyer who will actually pay your price. Or the dealer could have actually sold your item for $140. This practice is particularly prevalent in the jewelry business. Once the item has been turned over to a consignment dealer, you have little control over its sale.

The best way to sell something may be to a private collector, especially when very valuable works are involved. Private sales are not publicized but more high price records have been broken this way than at auctions.

Private sales are also the best way to sell memorabilia and collectibles. You can sell your material directly to collectors or through newsletters and other specialty publications. Many art and antique magazines have pages devoted to private sale offerings. You can also take out an advertisement in your local newspaper's classified section. If you decide to try this method, spend enough money to buy sufficient ad space and say as much as possible to attract potential customers.

If your item is particularly unique or valuable, you would probably do well to go to an agent. An agent's specialty is to match your item with an appropriate buyer—one who is experienced in the nuances of the art and antiques market. Because an agent works on commission, he is motivated to find a buyer willing to pay the highest possible price. This affords you the best opportunity to increase your profit potential.

An agent normally charges 10% of the selling price, taken from the owner. On extremely costly items or on a large number of items, the agent will sometimes charge a smaller commission.

To find a knowledgeable and reputable agent, seek recommendations from museum curators, gallery owners, antique shop proprietors, or specialized collectors' groups.

You should know that the major auction houses will not accept items that are worth less than $100. As a rule of thumb, the preeminent auction houses deal only in the upper end of the market that will benefit by extensive marketing, which is paid for by the owner of the object to be sold. And figure on a 10% commission to the house.

Should you consider taking your valuable pieces for sale at auction? By all means—they may be worth more than you think.

One of my clients told me of a friend who had an old silver bowl he was about to give to a thrift shop. He prodded his friend to try one of the most famous auction houses "just for curiosity's sake." An expert there identified the bowl as early 18th century American. It was subsequently sold at that auction house for $12,500!

Take your object to any place where you can gain accurate information about its origin, provenance, and value. For example, an expert in an auction house will examine the piece free of charge to determine if the house will offer it for sale. If the object is too large to bring in, other arrangments might be made. If you live too far away from a large auction house, they can make a judgement based on a good photograph along with your best description, its provenance, and any other pertinent information.

If the piece is accepted for auction and you agree to let it be sold, you must then agree to the terms of sale. Auction houses generally charge a minimum of 10%, but sometimes as much as 25%. Auctions might also have hidden costs: The seller often picks up the tab for cataloguing, shipping, and insurance. In addition, you may have to pay a minimum fee plus handling charges which can run from $50 to $200 even if your item was not sold.

Keep in mind, too, that at an auction you have to settle for the last bid, no matter how low it may be. An exception is if the house allows you to set a minimum, or reserve, price. If the item does not sell for the reserve price, the piece will be withdrawn, but in most cases, you will have to pay a percentage of the reserve price to the auctioneer.

Local auctions are the best market for less costly items. Because there is less (and sometimes no) advertising, a small catalogue (usually just a mimeographed list of items to be sold), and reduced related costs, it makes more sense for the average person to sell here. This frequently permits a bargain opportunity for the buyer, too.

Investigate all alternatives in order to get the best price. Don't give your item outright to the first buyer unless you are desperate to sell. Go to several knowledgeable dealers in your area. Find out what each will offer you and sell to the highest "bidder."

Here's a story illustrating this point. A woman wanted to sell an old doll with a porcelain head. An antique dealer offered her $800. A friend suggested she get a "second opinion" so the woman took the doll to a major auction house. The house specialist immediately recognized that the doll was made by a famous late 19th century French dollmaker. The doll was later sold for $8,000 at an auction.

Another major element in the art and antiques market is the estate sale. Generally, an estate sale takes place when, for any variety of reasons, a household must be liquidated. Usually the circumstance is the death of a parent who leaves an estate that is mostly furnishings—china, decorative objects, glassware, furniture, etc.

Items are priced on the low side because of the circumstances of the sale. It is a stressful time for the sellers and often a distress sale situation. Many times there is no will, cash must be raised to pay taxes, and heirs are in disagreement. Furthermore, one has to count the number of people who must be paid out of the sale, including administrators, executors, lawyers, as well as auctioneers or agents who are taking a percentage off the sale of the estate property.

Professional liquidators often charge a flat fee, but some charge a percentage of the gross sale, usually 15% to 25%. It is important to know and trust those people in charge of selling the estate material. Make sure they are licensed, where required, and legally registered.

Unfortunately, there is no simple solution. If one must sell immediately, the estate may only end up with 35% to 50% of fair market retail value.

Therefore, if there is no urgency to sell, you can stake a greater profit by slow, careful sales. In other words, hold onto the material until you can arrange for a satisfactory transaction.

Considering today's market, if you are in a high income bracket and you don't need the immediate cash, it may be much more profitable to *give* your material away to a college, church, or charity. This can offer a great tax advantage when properly handled.

Gift value to a deserving charity or other non-profit institutions is worth 100% to 120% of fair market retail value whereas selling an item outright may yield less than 50% of its value. To add insult to injury, you would be required to pay capital gains tax on any measurable sale. In terms of profit, donating your merchandise as tax deductions can result in a greater financial gain than selling.

If you decide to take this approach, be sure to have the bill of sale and/or appraisal statement to present to the IRS. It is also helpful to have a good photograph and accurate documentation of provenance and authenticity. In addition, with a very valuable item, it would pay to have a second appraisal opinion.

When selling, cash is preferable. Sometimes, however, you may be in a position where you have to take a check. Recognized dealers and auction houses will generally insist on writing you a check, and most people don't like to carry around large amounts of cash. A cash-only policy may result in a lost sale if the buyer is the spontaneous sort. If he has to go to the bank to withdraw the necessary funds, he may just decide it's not worth the effort.

Do you have to report the money you make on your sale to the IRS? If you sold the item for more than you paid for it, you have capital gain which legally must be reported on your income tax form. However, if the item is sold at a loss, the answer is generally no (unless the loss is great enough to reduce your taxable income).

In conclusion, you can sell successfully at a profit, but much depends on how quickly you must raise cash and to what extent you involve yourself in finding the best market. Your best chance for a profit begins by making sound and proper investments when buying. So pick your favorite area and learn enough about it and the marketplace to become a knowledgeable investor. If you're really serious about collecting and selling antiques for a profit, look for:

- perfection

- quality

- authenticity

- rarity

Conserve your resources and buy only the best you can afford. It will pay in the long run.

Like many people interested in collecting, I have motivation and enjoy making a profit. Yes, I'd like to make a million selling what I have collected over the years. But that's a fantasy.

The reality is that collecting can be highly speculative as a form of financial investment. That is why I tell my clients who come to me for advice in buying art, antiques, and collectibles that profit should be secondary to pleasure. Buy an item for its aesthetic appeal and only if you like it, because if it fails to make money, you'll still be able to enjoy your purchase.

There is only one sure way of winning: Buy what you personally treasure, treat it with tender loving care, and hopefully, when and if the time comes to sell, you'll turn a decent profit.

CHAPTER SEVEN

How to Get the Most from Auctions

Few human events spark the excitement, passion, and drama of an auction sale. There's always a thrill in bidding and hearing the sound of applause when the hammer falls—"Sold!"

Buying at an auction becomes a desire to possess, a search for identification, a driving force to succeed against another bidder. Whether you compete for a used toaster or a million dollar painting, an auction can be as stimulating as a shot of adrenalin.

An auction situation is basically a three-cornered fight among the owner of the property to be sold, the auctioneer, and the buyers. It's a conflict, sometimes a raging conflict, over possession. It's raw competition in its simplest form, but with all the complexities of human variations.

People are frequently so carried away by the excitement of the moment that they pay exorbitant prices for very little.

Some time ago, when I was in the process of appraising art works in the estate of William Randolph Hearst, he decided he wanted a particular painting about to be auctioned in London. I did a little research and learned that the portrait was worth about $4,000 to $5,000.

In my opinion, the work was not particularly good, but Hearst very much wanted to have it and sent his agent to England to bid for it. After the auction, the agent reported back to California. He was perspiring and appeared very nervous.

"Well, did you get the painting?" asked Hearst.

Stammering, the man replied, "Yes, but I paid $46,000 for it."

I had expected Hearst to become furious, but instead, he began to giggle and the giggle grew into a laugh. In fact, he couldn't stop laughing, for he'd sent two agents over and they had been bidding against each other!

As a postscript to the story, Hearst fired the man who didn't get the painting.

Hearst was a man of tremendous wealth, so perhaps he could readily find the humor in this situation. Yet bidding duels are common. It's easy to get caught up in the excitement of the moment. I've seen husband and wife so eager to buy something together that they've unwittingly started bidding on top of each other and end up paying two or three times the item's value.

Auctions are not for the insecure or naive. Even sophisticated auction goers can be taken in by stings, cons, hustles, and plain honest errors. Before you raise your hand for that first bid, it's advisable to become initiated in the rules of the auction arena. There are certain definite guidelines for buying at an auction, whether you are bidding a quarter or a quarter-million.

Here are 10 steps to help ensure your success at auctions:

1. ATTEND THE AUCTION PREVIEW

Most auction houses offer a preview period, often called an exhibition. This may be set for several hours or several days before the appointed time of the auction sale. The purpose of the preview or exhibition is to give the potential buyer the opportunity to see what is being auctioned and to examine carefully any particular item he may be interested in.

Merchandise at auctions represents the gamut of quality, authenticity, materials, scarcity, etc. The major auction houses will undoubtedly weed out most of the secondary merchandise before the sale. However, there are never any guarantees, therefore it's best to see the material in question with your own eyes.

The major auction houses also offer expert help during the preview period, allowing the buyer to ask detailed questions about any item for sale. These house experts can also offer consultation, information, and advice about the auction sale itself.

2. EXAMINE THE MATERIAL

Once you have set your eye on one or more items, inspect thoroughly. Make sure the drawers of that desk work. Study the wood and the craftsmanship of that cabinet. Examine each dish in a set of dinnerware, checking to make sure none is chipped or that an imitation has not been slipped in. Open the piece up, turn it upside down, sit on it. If you are considering a large piece, measure it to see if it will fit *before* you bid. Use your flashlight and magnifying glass to detect any flaws.

Then make careful notes about the item's dimensions, descriptions, number of pieces, and condition. This is done for future evidence in case your 100-piece silverware set arrives missing two knives and a serving spoon, or your Chippendale armchair comes with a mismatched cushion, or your perfect oak armoire is delivered with a dent in its door.

Don't feel awkward or self-conscious about examining the material or taking detailed notes. Legitimate houses encourage their customers to inspect goods to be sold. Take your time checking out every object on which you consider bidding.

3. STUDY THE CATALOGUE

Well before an auction, most of the larger houses will publish an illustrated catalogue of all the items to be included in the sale, as well as estimates for each item up for bid. You can buy the catalogue at the time of the preview exhibition or have it mailed to you. Catalogues are also available for perusal in the exhibit hall.

Catalogues can range in price from free (if mimeographed sheets are distributed) to $25. In the case of an important international sale, the catalogue can be an impressive hardcovered, full-color volume costing from $35 to $75 and up. These in themselves can become collector's items. Hardcover catalogues indicate a first-class auction with corresponding high-dollar sales.

Read and study the catalogue in detail, paying close attention to the catalogue description. Note if your object is listed as an original or a reproduction. If the full name of the artist and the date are part of the listing, you can assume there has been a documentation of provenance or an authentication of sorts. If, however, the painting is described as "School of Bernini," it is not a Bernini, but is thought by the auctioneer to be a painting by one of his students or admirers (or imitators).

I remember an old auctioneer in Manhattan who sold paintings with no documentation of provenance or authentication, but would list them in his catalogue as, say, "Genuine, Original School of Rembrandt." Obviously these were forgeries, but he sold them, and at a good price, too.

Interpreting the listings is another acquired skill. Catalogue writers are paid for their creative talents: An object of no particular style, provenance, or quality must be made to seem as if it possesses extraordinary beauty, historical association, and extreme rarity. Without quite misrepresenting the truth, a catalogue description may contain flowery phrases perfumed with foreign words. Often, the more flattering the description, the more ordinary the object it may be attempting to disguise.

It is important to note that almost none of the auction houses' catalogues will list the item's condition. It's up to you to spot the scratches, missing parts, or repairs. Beware of anything in the catalogue that says "as is." No matter how small the damage is, it will become more obvious to you with time. Now, you may get used to it—like you can get used to a toothache. For me, "as is" means the item is going to become more irritating as time passes. Aim for perfection.

Be sure to take the time to read the "terms of sale" usually typed in small print at the front of the book. Terms of sale include the percentage received from the seller of the object and the commission taken from the buyer (customarily 10% of the final bid price). The terms of sale also define the auction house's disclaimers. For example, the house is not responsible for damage during delivery, accuracy of auctioneer's pitch, the item's history or provenance, and whether the object was forged or stolen. These essential caveats of the game may be couched in obscure terminology and interminably long sentences, but it is important to understand the terms of sale before buying.

If you buy, be sure to keep a copy of the catalogue. It will serve as authentication and add some degree of provenance, which can increase your item's future dollar value.

4. DON'T FEEL BOUND BY ESTIMATES

Most catalogues will list an estimate of what the auction house's experts think the item will sell for. Don't believe it and don't be influenced by it. Estimates are not an accurate measure of the item's value and do not necessarily predict what the item will actually sell for.

An estimate may be placed far too high because a powerful seller has demanded a high "reserve price"—a minimum figure set by the owner. Conversely, an estimate may be too low because the house expert doesn't recognize what he has or underestimates the demand for the item. Sometimes something as unpredictable as bad weather will lower actual selling prices.

To give you an example of how extremely difficult it is to place an accurate estimate, I was acting as an agent for a client who wanted me to bid for a pair of demi-lune cabinets with an inlay crest of arms as a design in the center of each cabinet top. The catalogue listed its estimated sale for $8,500. I felt that because of their excellent condition and because they were a pair, my client should be prepared to have me bid up to about twice that amount. As it turned out, an English family, whose ancestors had the cabinets made with their own crest, wanted them returned to their rightful home and bid $125,000 to get them.

5. SET YOUR OWN PRICE LIMIT

No matter how badly you want an item, set a price limit in your own mind, rise to it if necessary, but don't go above it. To set your own price, use your judgment and knowledge of the field, determine the item's condition and quality, and figure out how much you are willing to spend for it. It's a good idea to have some shopping experience. (In other words, *know the market.*) What might the piece be worth at retail? How much might it be worth to a dealer if you decide to resell? You can glean this sort of information from antique shows, by shopping at various outlets that carry that kind of material and, obviously, by becoming something of an expert. Once you set your price limit, write it down with your notes on the item. Do this before you enter the auction floor; it will help you to stick to your estimated figure.

This may seem to take all the fun and spontaneity out of the bidding process, but believe me, that's the only way to win at an auction. Too many people are swept up in the bidding fever and end up badly burned.

I realize that it's easy to say to yourself, "I'm already up to my limit, what's another 10% more?" If you're that much in love with the item or it means that much to you, well, another 10% is not going to hurt. Just don't go higher than that, or before you know it, you'll be 50% or 100% over your limit.

Also, be aware of your own motivation. Are you exceeding your limit because you truly desire the object, or are you suddenly caught up in a oneupmanship game with the bidder next to you? Once the competition turns into a psychological game, the price ricochets higher and higher and the only real winner is the seller. Second place goes to the one who lost the bid. The loser is the person who now has the honor of paying an inflated price for an object he may not really want.

My general advice remains that you shouldn't go above the price you've set in your mind before the bidding begins. If you don't get the object you want this time, there will always be another auction. Maybe next time you'll find something even better with less competition and at a lower price.

If you are compulsively competitive or highly excitable, don't attend the auction yourself. Send a cool-headed friend who enjoys auctions and is willing to follow your instructions.

You may also want to consider hiring an agent to bid for you. An agent will understand the modus operandi of successfully buying at an auction, but will charge 10% of the sale price for his expertise. If you're bidding for an item of real importance, it's definitely advisable to get an outside opinion by an appraiser or a specialist who will act as your agent. Nelson Rockefeller, for whom I did much work, retained half a dozen people to advise him on any given purchase. He didn't want to be taken for any more than the *average* person would.

You can find an agent to bid for you through recommendations from museums, galleries, local antiques dealers, or from the auction house itself.

Another alternative, if you lack the discipline to bid sensibly, is to bid by mail or phone. These "order bids," as they are called, allow you to state an opening bid and a closing bid. These are then carried out by a house staff member who will bid as you specify to secure the object. Frequently, the opening bid at an auction is based on an order bid. The legitimate auction houses will respect your bid and go no higher. In fact, the order bid frequently obtains the object at a much lower price than the buyer had been anticipating to spend.

You can place an order bid whether or not you attend the auction yourself. But try to get to the preview exhibition, even if you can't be there to bid in person. If you have given an advance order bid, and you attend the auction after all and decide to bid, be sure you have cancelled your written bid or you may find you're bidding against yourself.

6. READY, SET, BID!

After you have attended the preview, examined the material, studied the catalogue, and estimated and set your price limit, you're ready to start bidding. Well, almost. The first rule in careful bidding is *never make the first bid.* You'll probably start the price higher than it need be. Remember, once the bidding starts, it can only go up. If you want the material badly enough, make the *last* bid, but never start the bidding process yourself.

The only exception to this rule is when no one else is bidding for the item. If nobody wants it, after a good length of time, offer half or a third lower than what the auctioneer is asking for. In other words, when the auctioneer says, "I want $20 for this tea pot" and the buyer response is silence, bid $10 or even $7.50.

On a recent weekend, I bought an exercise bicycle this way. I saw this particular type of cycle advertised in *The New York Times* for $275. The auctioneer was asking $100 for it. Nothing.

No takers. So, partly as a joke, I opened the bidding at $25. To my chagrin, no one else bid after that and I ended up with it.

The usual manner of bidding is to raise your hand or identification paddle. It is also accepted practice to speak your bid in a clear voice. Of course, there are numerous variations. Occasionally, bidders will have pre-arranged signals with the auctioneer to start or stop bidding. These signals might include holding an ear, folding one's arms, or some other subtle gesture.

Christie's, New York. Paddle being held at auction. Photo credit: Ted Cowell

Therefore, if you're not bidding on anything, *sit still.* Don't fidget or scratch your nose or you may end up owning the piece because the auctioneer takes your movement as a bid.

Again, in terms of bidding, stay out of duels. Don't get involved with another fellow and don't break into a bidding battle between two other bidders. When duelers openly reveal their eagerness, they merely succeed in raising prices, often beyond the bidder's means. Remember, the auctioneer is also a player in this game and it's to his advantage to prod prices higher by egging on two duelers.

Another important lesson: You have to be alert and move fast. The average bidding situation on a small item takes less than a minute. There may be 100 to 300 items for sale in a few short hours, so the auctioneer must move rapidly from one item to the next. He can only afford to spend time on the more expensive pieces in proportion to their importance or buyer interest.

In addition, at major international sales, you may not only have to compete with fellow buyers in the room, but also with people bidding by telephone or closed-circuit television.

In any case, if you want to win your bid, move fast and don't hesitate. While you are pausing to decide whether you can afford to go higher, the auctioneer may bring down the hammer—Sold!—to someone else's bid.

Listen attentively to what the auctioneer is saying. Unless you are a specialist in one or more subject matters, he frequently knows more about the material in question than you do.

But there is another reason to listen carefully. I remember an auction in Southampton, New York, where the auctioneer, in starting his sales pitch, said for all to hear, "genuine sterling silver"—and almost unheard, added "plate." As I listened even more attentively, there were several other items at the sale that he was not presenting honestly.

This is an example of fraudulent auctioneering. It is not a common occurence, but it happens often enough to be noticed, particularly at small country auctions. You would not find this unethical practice at a major, legitimate auction house.

Still, on rare occasions, the major house may present something that is honestly thought to be authentic, but is not. In any case, it's "buyer beware." Know your merchandise and have it appraised and authenticated rather quickly after you buy it.

7. BE PREPARED FOR SLEEPERS AND REPEATERS

The alert bidder must be prepared for "sleepers." These are items for which there is no competition. It may be a painting that's dirty, possibly a painting nobody else noticed or one behind a stack of other paintings. It may be a clock that doesn't work, but you happen to repair timepieces as a hobby. The silver bowl may lack authentication or have an obscure touchmark, but you have reason to believe it's the real thing.

Sleepers also occur if too many items of the same type are being sold in one auction. This situation has a great tendency to depress the market. By the fifth crystal vase, buyer interest may be lagging, but that may be a genuine Lalique vase you buy for much less money than it's actually worth.

If an item is not being bid on for one reason or another, take a chance if you have a use for that object or have an intuition about its value. Experience has shown that of all buying circumstances, bidding for sleepers at auction most frequently produces bargain winners.

Related to sleepers are "repeaters." Repeaters at auction are items that failed to sell the first time around. If you go to an auction several times and see an object being presented for sale for the third time, there is probably something seriously wrong with it.

Occasionally, a repeater could turn out to be a sleeper, because each sales offering would lower the price until eventually the item could turn out to be a bargain. Perhaps the item was overlooked because it was seen too often and other buyers lost interest. Or perhaps it was a chair with three and a half legs and you needed one not to sit on but merely to decorate a corner.

8. SENSE THE AUCTIONEERING METHOD

Auctions are not put together at random. Items are not presented in mere alphabetical order. Instead, good auctions are orchestrated. The house tries to arrange the order of sales to build to a crescendo of excitement and higher prices.

The auctioneer usually places the most important sales item or items at approximately the midway point of the sale when the crowd is largest and has been "warmed up." The major item is rarely sold at the end, because most people don't want to sit through an entire auction of lesser objects in order to buy the baby grand or master painting at the end of the sale.

By understanding the orchestration of the auction, you can determine which are considered to be the most valuable pieces and which items may turn out to be sleepers. After the "star" item is sold, the crowd may dwindle, leaving less competition for that mahogany table being presented at the end of the sale. By the time of the auction's denouement, other buyers may have already spent all they could, further reducing competition and increasing your chances of buying the object at a lower bid.

Also, observe the auctioneer. Learn his idiosyncrasies in selling. Is he slow at the start of the auction, encouraging duels, or allowing considerable moments to pass before hammering a sale? Conversely, is he selling fast, eager to move on to more important merchandise? If it's a long sale, is he tiring and slowing down toward the end? Or is he getting impatient to sell faster in order to quickly conclude the auction?

By paying attention to the ebb and flow of the sales, you can time your bidding accordingly.

9. "SOLD!"—PAYING AND ACCEPTING DELIVERY

You've just bid $230 for an eight-piece Wedgwood china serving set. The auctioneer's hammer slaps down, "Sold!" and it's yours. The last bidding figure is termed "hammer price." This is what you will pay to the auction house plus a 10% fee.

Cash is always a preferred means of payment, but a legitimate auction house will take a check if you have proper identification. In fact, most of the major houses will accept national credit cards. The large houses often have their own charge accounts.

The buyer is responsible for delivery. Unless you can carry your purchase home, you have to pay to have it transported to your home. Larger auction houses can arrange shipping for you, but if you are at a country auction, be prepared by bringing a station wagon or a pickup truck. (This is one way to find a bargain in large pieces—other potential buyers may not have the means to get them home and therefore do not bid.)

If your item is being delivered, be sure to inspect it closely before accepting it. Anything can happen to it between the exhibition showroom and your living room. If you've read your "terms of sale" carefully, you probably noted that the auction house assumes no responsibility for your item once the auctioneer's hammer falls.

10. IF SOMETHING IS WRONG

Let's say you've just accepted delivery of an 18th century mahogany secretary desk you bought at an auction for $4,000. You've taken it to be appraised and it turns out to be a reproduction made in 1940 and is valued at $650.

What can you do?

The first step is to stop payment on your check or withhold payment on your account if it's not too late.

Next, call the auction house in question and explain the situation. Make arrangements to have them re-examine the item either there or in your home. If you are dealing with a major auction house and they look at the piece and recognize their mistake, they will refund your $4,000.

In other circumstances, there may be some question as to whether you or they are right. If there is an honest dispute, the legitimate house will offer the piece for sale again and see what happens. You will then be refunded the hammer price and will not be charged any commission for selling it.

Now, if the same thing happened at a local auction house, let's say in a barn somewhere, you'd probably have little chance for retribution.

On the other hand, if you get no satisfaction from the auction house and you feel you've been bamboozled by gross misrepresentation or false advertising, you can receive assistance from your city's Department of Consumer Affairs.

Finally, your only recourse may be to bring a lawsuit against the auction house.

Beyond these measures there is little the unfortunate buyer can do. The auction house has pretty much protected itself by small print disclaimers in its catalogue and on the invoice you've signed.

Fortunately, most of the time buyers don't run into this type of problem. Many states have comprehensive regulations governing auction information and behavior; and several recent successful lawsuits have prompted more careful representation and handling by the majority of auction houses.

To recap the 10 rules of successful auction buying:

1. Attend the auction preview.

2. Examine the material thoroughly.

3. Study the catalogue in detail.

4. Don't believe catalogue estimates.

5. Set your own price limit and stick to it.

6. Never make the first bid.

7. Be prepared for sleepers and repeaters.

8. Be aware of auction orchestration.

9. Inspect merchandise closely before acceptance.

10. Have valuable material appraised—notify the auction house immediately if there is a discrepancy.

To conclude this chapter by telling you only of the legitimate, honest auction practices would leave the reader with an incomplete and inaccurate version of the whole picture. There are sometimes unscrupulous dealings. Knowing about auction chicanery will make you a more savvy bidder.

One of the most infamous arrangements is the bidding "ring." Let us assume there are six dealers at an auction along with all the other bidders. These dealers agree to form a ring. They jointly decide to buy certain items. Then they appoint one member of that ring to do the bidding, and the rest do not compete at the sale. This serves to eliminate competition between them, enabling them to obtain the object for a much lower figure than if they were bidding independently against each other.

Then, after the auction sale, the ring meets again and holds a second private "auction" where the merchandise is bid for among them.

These rings change every day, from auction to auction. It all depends on who has the money, and who wants what. They're shrewd and experienced people; the ring works very effectively and profitably for them. Because rings interfere with free competition, a reputable auctioneer will throw these people out as soon as he recognizes that a ring has been formed.

Observe the people around you. If you see a group of people at the back of the room shaking hands, exchanging signals, or even arguing among themselves, you know you are dealing with a ring. You'll see this more often at secondary auction houses.

Another example of something to be aware of the secret "reserve" price. A reserve price is the minimum price the seller will accept. In a secret reserve bid, the public is not aware a minimum has been set. Usually the secret reserve is unrealistically high. If it is not reached—and it frequently is not—the auction house agrees to "buy back" the item, thereby establishing an artificial sales price. In reality, the item is returned to the seller who pays a 5% commission to the auctioneer.

There have been numerous instances of auction items being manipulated to show an artificially high value. For example, a man owns a Van Gogh he decides to donate to a local museum for a tax write-off. A high reserve price "bought in" by the house provides written evidence of "established market value" on his tax return.

Reserve prices are also useful to raise the value of modern artists' work. There are many examples of contemporary work bringing in five times the money of comparable works. Research has proved that these high auction prices were a "buy-back" device being used to establish a theoretically higher fair market price through auction, providing a base value for large tax advantages to specific doners.

This practice is also considered good public relations by the artist's patrons and dealers and helps to develop the prestige and acceptance of the artist.

The only legitimate side to reserve bidding is that it protects the seller from the humiliation of selling a cherished item for far below what he believes it is worth. Sometimes the auctioneer himself will set a minimum when the work is established and recognized for a certain value. I can recall once acting as an auctioneer for a charity fundraiser in which a Picasso lithograph was being offered. I set the minimum for $500, but there were no takers. Rather than take reduced bids, which would have been insulting to the owner donating this work to charity, not to mention to Picasso's genius, I withdrew the lithograph from the sale.

There is nothing illegal about reserve prices, but they can be unethical when used to establish falsely high prices. I know several auctioneeers who won't accept reserve bids at all.

You can sometimes determine whether an item you are interested in is reserved by asking the auctioneer or looking at the catalogue. If the catalogue states "unrestricted sale," there may not be reserve bidding. Frequently though, catalogues don't specifically say that, and the auctioneer can't be depended on to mention a reserve.

There are also "fake bids." The auctioneer may clip off escalating prices at a rapid pitch, simply drawing bids out of the air. Buyers caught up in the excitement may not realize the prices are rising higher than are the actual bids. This is a completely phoney practice, but there is little the average buyer can do. If you follow my rule and don't go above your own set price, you won't lose your shirt in a fake bid situation.

One last point: Don't be deceived by the popular misconception that the "hammer price" is "fair market price." Auction value can in no way be construed as fair market retail value. A Louis XV commode a buyer practically "stole" for $6,000 at auction will seldom fetch even half that if he later tries to sell it to a dealer.

Furthermore, listing only an auction price for a tax deduction is often a good way to get yourself audited by the IRS. As I have stated earlier, in theory, auction value is statistically at best 65% to 75% of retail value.

Making money or getting a bargain is rarely the main pleasure of buying at an auction. The excitement, the competition, the thrill of winning out over an opponent is tremendously stimulating. It's a heady experience, but that feeling has also emptied the pocketbooks of buyers who end up paying more than they had anticipated for items they don't really want.

Therefore, I reiterate my rule encompassing all buying situations: Buy what you like and what you need. In auctions, follow the 10 guidelines presented here and you'll succeed in getting the most pleasure and value in your bidding ventures.

CHAPTER EIGHT

How to Avoid Fakes, Forgeries, and Other Phonies

Several years ago, I was asked to appraise a painting purchased at a public auction house for $6,500. The owner was under the impression he had bought a Goya. The sale was accompanied by a certificate of authentication. In addition, the painting was described and illustrated in a Goya biography that was included in the sale as further proof of authentication. I had a hunch the painting wasn't an original. I did an extensive research study and found I just happened to have the same art book in my library. It was the kind of high quality volume with the illustrations not printed on the pages, but rather lightly glued (tipped in) to a page accompanied by a printed description facing the illustration. When I opened my book to the page in question, the illustration was clearly not the same as in the other art book. The dealer had very cleverly taken a photo of the fake Goya, had it reproduced, removed the correct illustration, and replaced it with the phoney picture.

Then I studied the painting itself and found it had been re-touched, mounted on period canvas, restored, and reframed. On the back upper corner of the original canvas was a sales number. In tracking this down, I discovered the painting had been sold four years before from the same auction house for $650.

What had happened was that a rather unscrupulous dealer pur-chased the painting, added about $1,000 worth of "improvements" and then resold the piece with phoney authentication, netting close to $5,000 on the sale.

The work was utterly and completely unauthentic. Even the pa-pers were forged. Now, this work was sold as a Goya, it seemed to have authentication, and was even examined by a specialist in the auction house. But it was not a Goya and the buyer had been taken. If the painting were legitimate, it would have been worth at least $35,000. Had the buyer researched the market before buying, he would have learned that one could not purchase an authentic Goya for so little.

Furthermore, a Goya is not likely to turn up unheralded at a pub-lic auction. More likely it would have been sold privately or offered to a museum.

The buyer undoubtedly figured he had a bargain. He should have known there is no such thing. Unfortunately, the marketplace runs rampant with fakes, forgeries, falsified authentication, hidden flaws, imitations, and reproductions passed off as the real thing.

Occasionally, the seller or the buyer makes an honest mistake in judgement. Usually, however, it takes two to tango: the unscrupu-lous seller who deliberately misrepresents the item, and the willing buyer who believes the pitch. The buyer may be seduced by fancy sales talk—"the prestige of owning an original" or "the only one of its kind." The buyer may also be ignorant of what he is purchasing. He may not recognize the signs of a fake even though they are star-ing right at him. Most often the buyer is motivated by ignorance and gullibility.

False authentication can be a real problem for the honest dealer and buyer alike. Provenance or documentation does not always guarantee authenticity. This is one very important reason to obtain the services of a good appraiser who specializes in verifying authen-ticity. As I mentioned previously, this type of work is much like de-tective work.

Beyond the scientific tests, chemical analysis, infrared light, spectography, etc., that are used to determine an object's age and material, the appraiser must also be familiar with the artist's work, style, inspiration, and technique.

Some time ago, I saw two paintings signed and supposedly done by Stuart Davis when he lived in Rockport, Maine. I'd appraised many individual items in his memorial exhibition at the Smithsonian Institution in 1965. While I hadn't known the artist personally, I knew he experimented with different styles and techniques during

*Stuart Davis fake, top.
Modified copy of "Salt
Shaker, 1931." Elmyr de
Hory's fake Bonnard, right.*

the "Maine" period of his life as he searched to develop his artistic ideas.

Careful study by microphotography and X-ray of the brush-strokes, pigments, and canvas of the two paintings in question showed pronounced structural differences. They were obviously either the work of another artist who attempted to paint in the Davis style, or they were forgeries. Subjectively, the imitator always lacks the direct quality of the original inspiration. In the case of the Davis imitations, the emotional quality of the brushstrokes was lost.

Scientifically, the appraiser has to be aware of what pigment, canvas, or material the artist used. When analyzing pigment, for example, it must be given microchemical, spectrographic, or microspectographic analysis to uncover its chemical structure. This is most informative in determining age, because certain pigments were not developed before a specific date. With wood, microchemistry and Carbon 14 testing can accurately date a piece to within 25 years of its origin.

Sometimes, though, a piece can be authenticated with just a little ingenuity. I once positively identified a sculptured clay head as being the work of 15th century artist Andrea Verrocchio. How did I authenticate it? In this case, I found a fingerprint in the clay that matched those on other works sculpted by the artist.

An intriguing facet of art forgeries is that the forger-artist will always include something of his own personality or his own technique in the piece he is doing. Sometimes it can't be helped. Brush-strokes, for example, are as individual as handwriting. Recognizing the "signature" stroke of the original artist will distinguish his work from that of an imitator.

Fakes, no matter how well executed, have very little value. For the purposes of teaching, however, a collection of imitations can have instructional value. I own a good forgery. In my studio there-hangs an excellent example of a very clever imitation (see illustrtion on page 113) which was purchased for several thousands of dollars by a gentleman from Portugal. A very beautiful portrait on a wood panel, identified as Wilhelm Moreel, a 15th century mayor of Brussels, the painting was thought to have been done in 1484 by Hans Memling. The work came with certification of authenticity.

My client ordered a thorough examination. I took a second X-ray

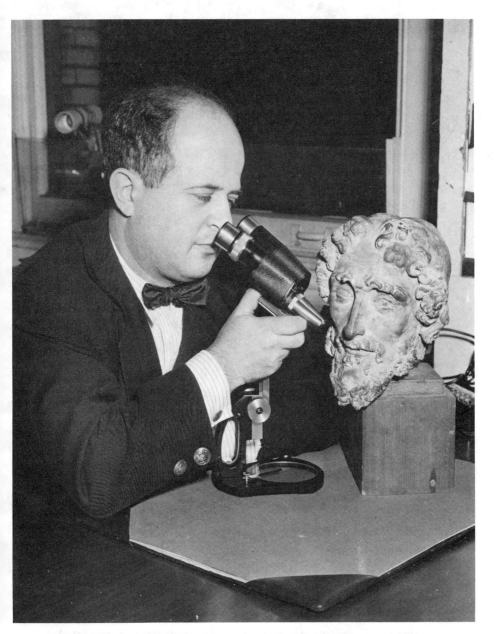

Rothschild examining genuine sculptured clay head by noted 15th Century artist, Andrea Verrocchio.

of it and found very little paint. The portion I examined under a microscope showed the "painting" was actually a biochromate photographic transfer. Furthermore, it is a perfect reverse image of the original which is in the Museum of Brussels.

This forgery was done by a process in which a gelatin-photographic image is slid off the glass and onto a properly-sized wooden panel. It was then baked, causing the glue sizing to produce a *craquelure* appropriate to the supposed age of the painting.

However, my client was not convinced. So I took a double X-ray—one of the painting and a second exposure on the same plate of a portrait of Mussolini. Mussolini came through quite clearly. My client laughed. He never did pay his bill, but left me the painting.

Recently the Metropolitan Museum of Art discovered that several gold vessels displayed in the Egyptian galleries were not from 1450 B.C., but were of recent manufacture. The discovery was made with a scanning electronic microscope which revealed that the inscriptions had not been done in the technique of the early Egyptians. The microscope also detected tiny hammer marks that should have softened or smoothed out over the centuries. The fakes have been removed for study by scholars.

Deliberate forgeries are rare. One should categorically separate the malicious attempt to imitate an artist from efforts at copies or reproductions. In classical times, many renowned artists had whole groups of apprentices who assisted on a painting, often retouching or filling in the work. In the case of Rubens, some of his apprentices actually painted more of the painting than did the master. Even today, a good artist-teacher will wind up with several students who have a tendency to imitate.

The lines dividing fakes, forgeries, and imitations are not black and white. To give you an example of the ambiguity sometimes involved, just recently I appraised a very interesting and beautiful Queen Anne tea table, supposedly American. After I carefully examined it under ultraviolet light, I saw that the legs had been re-carved much more recently—what was originally a simple provincial kind of table had been refined. The wood was authenitc, but an artisan had skillfully thinned the legs to make them more delicate. It was an old piece, but this deliberate upgrading, from my standpoint, made it a forgery, even though the basic material without modification was original.

*The Mayor of Bruges,
1484. The original, top,
painted by Hans Mem-
ling. The fake, bottom,
made through a biochro-
mate photographic transfer,
which is why it is a per-
fect reverse image of the
original.*

There is nothing wrong with a reproduction if it is sold as such. Numerous furniture manufacturers in this country and abroad specialize in high quality reproductions. Museums, too, sell jewelry and objets d'art that are excellent copies of the original. As long as the item is marked and identified as a reproduction, it has a certain value although it will never be as valuable as the original. There is a problem, however, if the mark is removed, covered, or ground off with the intent to pass the item off as an original. Unfortunately, this happens.

Therefore, it's advisable to have any valuable piece authenticated by a specialist. As previously noted, Nelson Rockefeller often obtained half a dozen opinions on one object. Although he employed expert buyers, he still was concerned with authenticity.

Another important identifying characteristic is the material used. I have already suggested that paintings can often be dated by the type of pigments used. The same is true of furniture. Certain woods were used in specific periods and specific styles. For example, when I see a Gothic piece of furniture made from spruce, I know automatically that it's not authentic because oak was the wood of Gothic times. Mahogany, walnut, and fruitwoods each have their own periods.

Each era also has its own original style, individual characteristics, and regional details. One can determine fairly accurately the artisan or manufacturer when these factors are considered along with the intrinsic materials used. Tool marks can also be identifying characteristics—are screws used? What about nails? Which kind of nails? Are the joining pieces hand-cut or machine cut?

Another element to consider in buying furniture is the degree or percentage of originality—how much of the chair is original? Has it got one new leg, two new legs, or has it been substantially repaired? In a set of chairs, how many are authentic and how many are exact reproductions?

Recently I appraised a set of six very nicely carved Queen Anne chairs. The only trouble was that four of the chairs were copies. They were exquisitely carved with great subtlety of style, but still, they were copies.

In this case, I was able to identify them by the tool marks. Only the two originals were made by chisel; the others had the tell-tale signs of power driven tools. Then I went one step further and looked at the chairs under ultraviolet light. The old chairs showed layers of varnish, whereas the new chairs didn't have this varnish depth.

There are all sorts of tricks known in the antique industry. I have even seen books sold on the market bearing titles such as *How to Fake Antique Furniture* and *The Gentle Art of Faking Furniture*. These are well-written, fascinating books, but they don't cover some of the really deceitful problems buyers face.

The arena of fakes and forgeries is complex. Fortunately, modern techniques make it simpler to determine the difference between a copy and an original. Whether we are dealing with furniture, paintings or any other creative endeavor that can be imitated, the most important tools in avoiding fakes and forgeries are knowledge and experience. The more information you have about a specific period, style, and artist, the less likely you'll be fooled.

This is why I advise my clients to take valuable purchases to an independent appraiser who specializes in authentication. A generalist or an auction appraiser may not have sufficient knowledge or experience. If an item has great financial value, too, don't depend on one person's estimate it's good to get a second opinion as well.

I can recall a rather notorious case of an appraisal overestimate. About 10 years ago, a major auction house appraised an antique candlestick for $130,000. It was believed to be owned by Catherine I of Russia who gave it to a church in the Kremlin around 1725. The candlestick was over five feet high and made of silver. Based on this appraisal estimate, the owner donated the candlestick to a museum and claimed a hefty tax deduction.

The IRS audited the owner and hired its own appraiser, who valued the candlestick at only $18,000. Finally, an independent specialist in Russian art was consulted. He concluded that the candlestick was merely a replica, had no historic significance, was of silver of a questionable quality, and was only worth $2,000 to $3,000.

Needless to say, the owner could have saved himself considerable expense, litigation, lawyers' fees, and headaches if he had had the candlestick properly authenticated and appraised from the start by a knowledgeable specialist.

Another serious problem is that of stolen materials. Unfortunately, auction houses have emerged as major vehicles for the sale of stolen art work. Part of the problem is that auction firms seldom ask to see proof of ownership. If you check the "terms of sale," you'll find that an auction house is not liable if it unknowingly sells a stolen painting. The auction house is not responsible for the accuracy of a painting's provenance.

Another part of the problem is that the police often have very little to go on in tracking down stolen pieces. Investigators say they constantly see stolen property notices describing the work as: "Stolen: One painting of seascape with lighthouse" or "Missing: One abstract sculpture of a female nude." Without a precise description or a good color photograph, the chances of identifying a stolen piece are virtually nil. So it is understandable that an auction house might fail to discover if items offered for sale are stolen.

If you should happen to innocently buy a stolen artwork at an auction that is later identified as such, you can probably kiss your painting—and your money—goodbye.

My best advice to minimize your risk is to buy only from reputable houses or dealers. The major ones usually provide a 30-day "grace period" (check the catalogue's terms of sale). You have that time to have the item appraised and authenticated. If it is not genuine and you have evidence to prove it beyond a shadow of a doubt, a legitimate house will most likely return your money. In a case of outright fraud, your only recourse may be to bring legal action against the consignor, if you can find him. In any case, it's "buyer beware."

Realistically, nobody is beyond making a mistake—it's a fact of life. But nobody likes being had. No matter how much you liked a piece or thought you needed it, if you later learn it's a phoney, you'll probably come to hate the thing. Its presence will be an irritating reminder of the money you lost (not to mention your personal fallibility).

How can you avoid getting taken?

1. Develop healthy suspicion. The rule of the game is "Buyer Beware!"

2. Don't take anything for granted, including certificates of authentication. When a lot of money is involved, get an immediate appraisal. If authentication is extremely important, get a second opinion.

3. Thoroughly examine the piece. Check for fiddling on dates, inappropriate materials, tools used, etc.

4. Beware of a seriously underpriced item. Remember, if you think it's a bargain, it's probably not.

5. Anything described as "Chippendale style" or "school of Rembrandt" is never the real thing.

6. Get in writing a detailed bill of sale. If you are buying an original, make sure the bill indicates this. It should also list any restorations done and period of manufacture.

7. Out-of-the-way country shops and auctions will never carry "long-lost masterpieces."

8. Watch out for imitations in the midst of originals.

9. Association does not necessarily make for value. Never buy a piece because George Washington once used it. Don't believe it for an instant. Historical myth is rampant in the antique business.

10. Buy only from reputable dealers. Their reputation is at stake along with your investment.

Knowledge is money. Study your area of interest whether it be coins, porcelain, furniture, stamps, books, or paintings. Read books on the period in question, and compare other items of the same period. Learn how much similar items are worth. Discover how rare or common a particular type of object is. Study the methods to determine material or age of the items in which you are interested.

Knowledge is money. Study your area of interest whether it be coins, porcelain, furniture, stamps, books, or paintings. Read books on the period in question, and compare other items of the same period. Learn how much similar items are worth. Discover how rare or common a particular type of object is. Study the methods to determine material or age of the items in which you are interested.

Find a trustworthy dealer. Get a good appraiser to authenticate your purchases. These are your most effective defenses against fakes, forgeries, and other phonies.

CHAPTER NINE

A General Guideline for Buying... Anything

Entire books have been written describing the qualities and values of just one type of item, such as movie posters, candlesticks, clocks, buttons, dolls, fans, bottles, china, clothing, furniture, or jewelry.

Individually, each collection or collectible category has its own variables due to the personal finances of the collector, opportunities to find material, the amount of available desirable material, and the ever changing tastes and interests of the collector.

Anything that you collect is a matter of your aesthetic interest in the item or the functional purpose it serves within your life. The acquisitive impulse is normal and enjoyable.

When you realize that values are constantly changing and that collectibles are never a sure financial investment, the most important factors in buying become desirability and utility. In other words, do you like it, and can you use it?

In fact, if I had to summarize the contents of this book, I would stress three vital rules that apply to everything and anything you may buy:

- Buy what you like.

- Buy what you can use.

- Buy perfect condition.

With these three rules firmly in mind, the following is a brief introduction to the major collectible categories:

Advertising

Anything distributed as premiums or advertisements in times past is selling well in today's market. This includes promotional buttons, trays, calendars, mirrors, jars, tins, and just about any item with an advertiser's logo. Mass production has reduced the desirability of many items because of the quantity still available and the lack of quality artwork on them. But some items are worthwhile as reflections of a given moment in time. World War I posters, or a Ronald Reagan movie poster will carry an especially good price. Watch out for copies—only the real thing can gain in value.

Americana

Loosely defined, Americana is historical material relating to a particular locality or period in time. Any Lincoln material continues to enjoy great interest among collectors as do items related to the Civil War. Any item depicting a particular event such as a centennial exhibition or a World's Fair is desirable.

Six antique advertising cards, 19th Century. Courtesy of the New York Historical Society. →

A GENERAL GUIDELINE FOR BUYING...ANYTHING

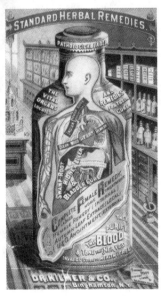

Double-wheel coffee grinder with handle;."Enterprise Mfg. Co., Philadelphia. USA" cast in base. From the collection of Mary Brandwein.

Applicances

Original patent models, early radios, phonographs, drink mixers, etc., can be popular collectibles. Anything made in Edison's studio, or Victor models, are particularly valuable. The appliance should be in good shape—no dents or damage. Check to make sure no parts are missing. Watch for frayed cords or plugs in bad condition. If the item doesn't work but you have the skills and desire to repair it, it may be a worthwhile investment. Remember, any common, domestic article used today will become valuable after passing through two generations.

Architectural Ornaments

These can often be had for free if you notice a building being torn down. Bring a wheelbarrow and cart away window shutters, fireplace frames, door hinges, or the whole door if you need one. Hotels or stores going out of business will sometimes advertise a "fixture sale" for everything from night tables to chandeliers. At antique shows, look for etched glass window panes, cast-iron American eagles, and ornate Victorian doorknobs or doorbells.

Autographs

Some are tremendously valuable when they reflect a socially or historically significant event. Prime examples are letters written by Washington and Lincoln. When considering the autograph of a modern personage, for example President Kennedy, be certain that the signature was made by hand and not by machine. Sought-after autographs include those of Marilyn Monroe, John Lennon, and Elvis Presley. Other autographs have specific interest for collectors in specialized categories.

Books

Look for hardcover first editions with their original dust jackets, both in perfect condition. Art books with plates will generally be more valuable. Watch out for dog-eared pages, broken bindings, missing pages, etc. All recent (1940 and on) books and paperbacks have no value other than the pleasure of reading them. Don't pay more than a couple of dollars for these.

Examples of dime novels, c. 1809-1900s.

Bottles

Bottle collecting is one of the foremost sub-categories of glassware collecting. Bottles are a highly desirable type of ornamental, decorative collection for the home. Look for Art Deco, Art Nouveau and other particular patterns that reflect a given moment in time.

Roman Empire bottles, part of a collection.

Boxes & Bins

Wooden boxes from the 19th century and on will have some collectible value. Some specialized items include tool boxes, cutlery
trays, grain bins, dough boxes, and jewelry cases. If the box is missing its lid, pass it up.

Buttons

Buttons are a highly desirable type of collectible. They were first
used in the mid-1600's and were usually made of jewels and gold.
By the end of the century, buttons became more common and were
made of silver, brass, and tin. Some are hallmarked, which adds to
their value. Artistically-made enameled and lacquered buttons from
the 18th and 19th centuries are particularly valuable. Gold and silver buttons, or really fine buttons made with semi-precious stones,
can be worth thousands of dollars.

Candlesticks

Good buys include Depression glass, hand-cut glass, and porcelain candlesticks. Other favorites are made of brass, pewter, wrought iron, and cast iron. A pair is more valuable than a single candlestick. Anything from the 18th century to the present will have value.

Chessmen

The modern form of chessmen came into being during the 12th century. Early pieces were carved in ivory, bone, and hardwood. The late 17th century produced chess figures in precious metals and jewels. By the 18th century, all types of materials were used: bronze, pewter, amber, agate, glass, and ceramics, including valuable sets by Doulton, Staunton, and Wedgwood. Look for originality of design concept, quality of the workmanship and, of course, a complete set.

Christmas Cards

People first began mailing out Christmas cards in the early 19th century. Styles included colored lithographs, frosted, religious, three-dimensional, even trick and joke cards. Anything from the last century in good condition is collectible.

Clothing

Best buys are from the 19th century to the 1920's. Examples might include a coat designed in 1910 by Paris designer Worth, a "Flapper" dress with a pointed hemline, and a hat by a well-known maker.

Coins

One of the outstanding categories of collectible material is coins, both from the standpoint of investment and as fundamental examples of historical association. The collecting of coins is one of the oldest hobbies in existence. Coins as we know them today date back to about 700 B.C. Coin collecting also affords the opportunity to learn about people. Imagine the thrill of holding in your hand coins that were in actual circulation during the time of Alexander the Great, Julius Caesar, Mark Anthony, and Cleopatra, and coins of the Bible such as the "widow's mite," the "shekel" and the "tribute penny." This hobby is international, but most Americans prefer to collect coins and money used in the United States. Some of the most interesting specimens in this group date back to the Colonial period and include the pinetree shillings of Massachusetts (1652), paper money issued to finance the Revolution, and the first coin authorized by the United States government in 1787, on which is inscribed, "We Are One" and "Mind Your Business." The king of coins is considered to be the 1804 dollar, which has been sold at auctions for over $75,000. The majority of coins can generally be purchased at fairly reasonable prices. There are certain fundamentals that should be kept in mind, however. The age of a coin does not always determine its value. Rarity is also very important, whether you're collecting American pennies or Egyptian gold coins. Never clean a coin by rubbing or scouring. In collecting coins, there is as much pleasure and interest in inexpensive coins as the higher priced ones. Gold coins, silver coins and much more easily recognizable paper money, have their own collectible categories, and as such require specialized study and care as to selection, condition, rarity, and of course, time and place of origin.

Comic Books

The older the better in this collectibles category. Classics such as "Mickey Mouse," "Donald Duck," "Popeye," "Superman," "Batman," and "Captain Marvel" are best. First issues are most valuable. Comic books must be in excellent condition.

Computers

Old computer components may become collectibles of the future. I have a computer board that's about 2' x 3' in size. The same material is now put on a chip smaller than my pinkie nail. The board may have great interest for the computer enthusiast. Computer parts are also being incorporated into jewelry by some avant-garde designers. These, too, may be valuable as a reflection of a period of time in our technological history.

Diamonds

In consideration of this most common but nevertheless valuable commodity, I recommend that if a person is interested in quality, purchases should be made in consultation with a reputable dealer who has training in gemology—preferably from the Diamond Trade Association—and who is a member of the National Association of Jewelry Appraisers. Diamond comes from the Greek word *adames* meaning indestructible. Diamonds are a pure form of carbon naturally crystallized and are the hardest substance known to man. Diamonds are 90 times harder than sapphires and rubies, the second and third hardest substances. Only diamonds can cut diamonds. Diamonds have the ability to reflect light and bend its rays at sharper angles than any other gem. In a cut and faceted diamond, light rays enter, pass through to planes beneath, are reflected back at sharp angles to other planes, and are multiplied by each reflection returning to the surface. This produces an extraordinary brilliant effect. Since the angle at which light rays are reflected can be measured, diamond cutting has been scientifically developed to produce the maximum of recaptured rays. Diamonds are graded and valued by four major criteria: carat, cut, clarity and color.

Carat or weight—One carat is equal to .20 grams and five carats are equal to one gram. A diamond weight gauge is used to determine the diameter and depth of the stone, which enables the appraiser to calculate the stone's weight. Today's stones are cut with the objective of obtaining maximum brilliance. Weight is of secondary importance. For example, three small perfect diamonds are much more valuable than one larger imperfect one of comparable weight.

Cut—Cut refers to the proportioning, faceting, and polishing of each stone. A diamond is cut for the maximum refraction and reflection of light. The "Brilliant Cut" originated in the mid-18th century and is still used today. This type of cutting has developed scientifically according to the laws of refraction to achieve maximum brilliance; a well-cut diamond has 58 facets. Cut also refers to the shape into which the diamond has been fashioned. The most popular cuts are round, emerald, marquise, oval, pear and heart. An old and simple cut of stone is called cabochon and was popular in the Middle Ages. A cabochon stone is polished round or oval in a convex shape rather than in facets.

Clarity—Standards are specific in the passage of light through the stone. There are 10 clarity grades. If a diamond is without blemishes such as carbon spots, cleavages, and occlusions under 10-power magnification, it is termed flawless. Flawless diamonds are relatively rare and are priced accordingly. Most diamonds used in jewelry have a few blemishes visible with 10-power magnification. These can be plotted and graded. The number of blemishes as well as where they occur in the stone affect value. Diamonds with blemishes that can be seen with the naked eye have greatly reduced value. Gemologist grade diamonds as seen under 10-power magnification in the following manner (G.I.A. grading):

F	—Flawless, no visible occlusions
VVS	—Very, very slightly occluded
VVS,½&	—Very, very slightly occluded
VS,1,2	—Very slightly occluded
SI,1,2	—Slightly occluded
IMP,1,2,3	—Imperfect

(The numerals indicate degrees of imperfection.)

Color—Colored diamonds occur in almost every shade of the rainbow. They are rare and as colored stones must be considered individually. The clarity and polished perfection of a diamond is its measure of value.

The trade distinctions for color are:

D,E,F	—Colorless
G,H,I,J	—Nearly colorless
K,L,M	—Faint yellow
N,O,P,Q,R	—Very light yellow
S to Z	—Light yellow
Above Z	—Fancy yellow

While a diamond with intense yellow color is called a "canary," diamonds which have fine clarity are called "fancy" stones and maintain the highest value.

Gemologist grade diamonds as seen under 10-power magnification in the following manner (G.I.A. grading):

F	—Flawless, no visible occlusions
VVS	—Very, very slightly occluded
VVS,½	—Very, very slightly occluded
VS,1,2	—Very slightly occluded
SI,1,2	—Slightly occluded
IMP,1,2,3	—Imperfect

(The numerals indicate degrees of imperfection.)

TYPES OF IMPERFECTIONS (Clarity Grading)

External	Internal
Cavity	Cleavage, Fracture, Feather
Nick	Included crystals (carbon spot)
Grain-Knot	Pin-Points
Natural	Cloud
Scratch/wheel marks	Knot
Extra Facet	Bearded girdle
Rough girdle	Internal Grain/Knot
	Laser Hole

Dolls

The doll originally was fashioned from a piece of wood or a few rags tied together to resemble, in a crude way, the human form. Many dolls have been found in Egyptian tombs. Other early dolls were made with wooden or wax heads on kid or linen bodies. Since then, dolls have been made from leather, china, porcelain, celluloid, rubber, papier mache, and today, plastic. Ancient dolls and those dressed in costumes representing various nations make interesting studies for the collector. One of the greatest collectors of dolls was Queen Victoria of England. As a result, dolls from this period are very popular. Nineteenth century American dolls are also popular, as are 19th century Bru dolls from France. Marseilles dolls (1890-1930) are also valuable. Look for a china head and manufacturer's name on neck or body. American 20th century (and up to the present day) dolls have some value, although less so since they are mass-produced. Popular styles are Shirley Temple, Kewpie, Barbie, and Brooke Shields dolls. Dolls must be in good condition. Make sure limbs, neck, etc. are easily movable. Beware of imitations. Material for this hobby is readily available to the collector and can be easily displayed in cabinets.

Fans

Fans are another very popular and decorative collectible. The earliest existing fans date back to the 16th century. The variety of styles is endless. Materials include gold, silver, feathers, ivory, mother-of-pearl, tortoise shell, sandalwood, silk, lace, and paper. Some were ornamented with jewels, gilding, and carved pearls. The Victorian period produced a great number of fans, many of them still available and affordable today. One of my good friends, Kate Smith, had a collection of over 2,000. Some were worth a lot of money, and of course this collection has added value because of its association with Kate Smith. Again, the rule of thumb is that any collection as a whole is more valuable than the sum of its individual parts.

Furniture

Books have been written exclusively on the art of buying used or antique furniture. In very broad terms, the best values are in oak and mahogany. Anything produced from the 1850's to the 1950's will have some value. In general, when buying furniture, check for high quality in construction and material. Take your time and double-inspect the piece, inside and out, preferably with a flashlight, to spot cracks, gouges, flaws, and missing parts. Very large pieces that are not in scale with contemporary settings can be bought for much less than small scale pieces. Poor condition also reduces value. Buy costly pieces only from established, reputable dealers.

American rosewood sofa, c. 1856-1861, top, left. Unrestored English Sheraton tambour-top satinwood desk cross banded with tulipwood c. 1780, appraised at $625, top, right. Early Jacobean ebony and oak court cupboard, ornamented with cushioned, panelled doors executed in ebony, bottom, left. English court cupboard, c. 1650, bottom, right.

Glass

Glass pieces vary widely in style, cut, and quality. Glass, even of ancient civilizations, is undervalued in the collector's market, so prices can be relatively low. Of the older glass, two popular collectible styles include ale, cider, or wine glasses made from the 1680's

American glass vase. Steuben, 1929, top. Hand pressed glass stemware by George Sakier, 1935, bottom. Made by Fostoria Glass Co.

and on. These were usually large and had a deep conical bowl. After the 1740's, these often had decorations of hops and barley, apples and blossoms, or grapes and vines. Very ornately designed cordial glasses were in vogue in the 18th century following the discovery of liqueurs. These are small-bowled with long, thin stems. Some of the most popular of the more modern styles are Victorian brilliant cut (1890-1915), Cambridge (look for letter "c" in a triangle on the bottom), Carnival (1900-1920), Cranberry (gold is added to the glass, producing a rich, dark red color), Depression (1930's), and 19th century glass (1825-1888). In general, look for hand-cut pieces identifiable by sharp edges. Check for names and dates etched on the bottom. Glass should have a clear ring when tapped. Avoid pressed glass imitations. Also watch out for "flash-coating," a thin layer of color over clear glass. Look for wear marks. The market is full of imitations, so if you are tempted to pay a top price, have it authenticated first. Automatically blown, or pressed and formed (most glass made after 1906) pieces such as milk or beer. bot tles, will sell for less. Older pieces, particularly if they're of an original design and signed by the artist, are more valuable. An ancient Roman glass vessel could be worth several thousands of dollars.

Gold

In Latin, gold is *aurum* meaning shining dawn. Since the origins of man, gold has been monetarily and romantically the most valuable of precious metals. Gold is also the softest or most malleable of metals. It is chemically inactive and is not affected by moisture, oxygen, or ordinary acids found in the earth or the air. Gold will not tarnish as does silver or copper, but is alloyed with such metals to harden it. Gold is also alloyed with platinum, nickel, and zinc. Pure gold is 24K or karat. 22K gold is 91.6% pure; 18K is 75% gold; the most popular, 14K gold, is 58.5% pure; and 10K is 41.6% pure. Although gold items will always have "melt-down" value, value is greatly enhanced by design, maker, and historical association.

Guns

Guns are primarily valued for their use, but in some cases they do become collectibles. Some antique models are quite rare. Eighteenth century guns are most desirable for individual collectors. If in good condition, old guns can run into the thousands of dollars.

Hourglasses

Originally known as sandglasses when they first appeared about 1720, the glass bulbs were held in frames of wood, silver, brass, or ivory. From 1760, the glass was blown as a single unit. Dating can be determined by the quality of the glass.

Indian Handiwork

Old baskets and rugs are most valuable and might sell in the hundreds of dollars. Items made between 1950 and 1970 will sell for much less. Contrary to popular opinion, a genuine Navajo arrowhead is only worth around $1.50.

Jewelry

Throughout the ages, people have used jewelry for many reasons, including self-adornment, ego satisfaction, and social position. Beyond these factors, jewelry has intrinsic or "melt-down" value simply because of the materials used—gold, silver, and precious stones. Value is added on by the quality of the design of the piece. Jewelry can also be identifiable by a designer's style, by its purity of line and form. Age, history, and association add to the value.

Victorian—The Victorian era is considered to date from 1837 to 1900. Look for heavy and ornate settings. Most were made in 9-, 10-, or 12-karat rose gold. Pendants, lockets, and pins were particularly popular in sentimental motifs.

Art Nouveau—From 1895 to 1930, jewelry turned graceful, light, and feminine. Designs were typically sensuous, flowing, and asymmetrical. Motifs included the shapes of semi-nude maidens, flowing entanglements of hair, swirling stylized flowers, and other wave-like designs drawn from nature. The intricacies of Art Nouveau design make it difficult to reproduce, but because it is currently fashionable, jewelry manufacturers are creating imitations. If you're more interested in authenticity than adornment, buy from a reputable dealer of estate pieces.

Art Deco—The period from 1925 to 1935 ushered in the geometric lines easily recognizable as Art Deco. Characteristic motifs reflect technology and speed—the "machine age." The simple, angular lines were easily mass-produced. (That was the idea.) Authentic pieces often used less expensive jewels or settings, such as

Lalique pin with jade and emeralds, c. 1930, worth $2,600 in 1969.

marcasites, instead of diamonds, aluminum instead of silver, so even the real thing could be affordable. Pieces range from an inexpensive black plastic bracelet to a pin with semi-precious stones.

Kitchenware

The big interest today is the "country look." Anything made from 1800-1950 will have some value. Look for butter churns, cookie cutters, griddle turners, rolling pins, coffee grinders, brass trivets, eggbeaters, copper teapots, and any item with advertising on it. You have to differentiate between mass-produced commercial pieces from mail-order houses and handmade country pieces. An item showing an element of style or period will have more value. A kitchen tool that was actually used may not necessarily have to be in perfect condition provided it still has some utility.

Lamps and Lights

Anything from the 19th century and on will have collectible value. Art Nouveau style lamps are particularly trendy. Tiffany types with a bronze base and a leaded glass shade will start in the low hundreds and, depending on quality, style and condition, will skyrocket. Authentic Tiffany pieces are astronomical in price.

Magazines
First issues are most valuable. They must be in good condition with no missing pages. Generally expect to pay no more than a few dollars for most magazines. Especially good buys are magazines with covers by noted illustrators such as Norman Rockwell and N. C. Wyeth. A premiere issue of "Playboy" with Marilyn Monroe on the cover will fetch several hundred dollars.

Marriage Souvenirs
These might include a pair of knives in a single sheath, drinking vessels of silver or pewter engraved with initials, fans with wedding motifs, ring pillows embroidered with the couple's names, or loving cups with names and the marriage date. Historical association is the most important factor in this category, but make sure the association with the historic characters can be authenticated.

Matchsafes
These are small boxes which serve the purpose of holding matches. They were largely replaced by cigarette lighters and matchbooks (which are also collected). Old matchsafes were made of anything from tin to porcelain to silver and gold. They frequently carried advertisement logos. Prices vary considerably.

Mechanical Banks
Always a popular collectible, the mid to late 19th century banks are most valuable. The bank must work to be worth collecting. These are widely copied, so watch out for tell-tale bargain prices.

Money Boxes
Today these are more commonly known as "piggy banks." Money boxes were first used in the 16th century and had to be smashed in order to obtain the contents. Designs included hens, barrels, pine cones, bee hives, and, of course, pigs. They were usually made of earthenware. The familiar thin horizontal opening for coins was introduced in the 17th century. Cottage shapes were popular in the 18th century. Needless to say, only intact boxes are valuable.

A collection of Matchsafes.

Music box, c. 1850.

Music Boxes

Driven by clockwork-like machines, these originated around 1800. The earliest ones have a weak, wobbly tone. A series of technical improvements allowed elaborate musical tones by 1820. Around 1850, drum and bell tones were introduced. Only handmade music boxes have any real value, as the latter half of the 19th century brought cheaply made, mass-produced items. The changing tastes of a culture can be seen in the boxes' outer designs and the choice of music.

Musical Instruments

Value will vary depending on use—a hopelessly out-of- tune zither with a floral decoration that might decorate a wall shouldn't go for much. Such things as an old bugle made into a lamp are not to my taste. Usable instruments are another matter. Any finely-made original musical instruments, including woodwinds, brass, and even organs, if in good condition, have tremendous value.

Needlework Items

Lace, such as doilies or tablecloths, varies greatly in price. It can be eminently affordable or out of reach for the average collector. Applique, in which fabric motifs are stitched to a contrasting fabric, is one of the oldest forms of textile ornamentation. Crewel work was popular in the late 17th century—work of the time had fantastic designs of flora and fauna. Crewel is distinguished by its intricate, complex, and wide variety of stitches. Samplers began in the 16th century and were probably "trials" to perfect stitching techniques. By the 18th century, these became children's showpieces. Although some are examples of fine needlework, others are simplistic and poorly done. Early 19th century American samplers, dated, with some degree of style and design, are usually good investments. Before investing any real money, make sure the piece is authentic.

Newspapers

Collecting newspapers and news clippings is a fascinating hobby and, in all reality, is the collecting of a day-by-day history of the world. Most valuable are newspapers related to major national events such as the Battle of Bull Run, McKinley's death, or those with huge headlines reading "War Declared on Germany." One of the greatest difficulties in collecting newspapers is that they deteriorate rapidly. Most newspapers are made from wood pulp; light and air affect them, causing them to turn brittle in just a few years. Very old newspapers, such as the British *Weekly Current* published in the 17th century, and the *Boston News Letter,* America's first newspaper published in the early 18th century, were made of paper composed of a rag and clay mixture. These, in most instances, are in a much better state of preservation than wood pulp papers issued 100 years later. The collector of newspapers may find material in old cellars and garrets. Old newspapers may still be purchased at comparatively small cost. It is a collection that requires some space for storage and display.

Paperweights

Very popular in Victorian times, they were designed as animals, reptiles, fruits, etc. Materials included metal, ceramics, and stone. In glass, paperweights achieved splendid aesthetic forms and design.

A collection of glass paperweights.

Patent Models

Original patent models used in the patent offices are highly desirable examples of inventive imagination and skill.

Pewter

Pewter is an alloy usually of tin and lead which was used in tableware until the effects of lead poisoning became known. Today, pewter is valued for its decorative purposes. Different grades of pewter showed various alloys; the best pewter was made of tin and copper. The collector of pewter has a long road to travel back in his study of this subject. Interesting specimens of pewter have been dug up in ancient Roman excavations and claim has been made that pewter was made in Asia and Asia Minor even before the days of Rome. Pewterware obtained its greater popularity during the the

Pewter beakers, American, c. 1750-1795.

15th and 16th centuries and continued to be used generally until the latter part of the 19th century. English pewterware was the most popular. Many fine candlesticks, ladles, flagons, tankards, spice boxes, plates, cups, lamps, and various kinds of spoons can still be found and testify to the craftsmanship of the pewterers of bygone days. There are also many fine pieces of old church pewter such as chalices, alms dishes, etc. American colonial pewterware ranked in quality and workmanship with that of England. Indeed, many of our original pewterers were English. Much of colonial pewterware is hallmarked in the same manner as silver, although it has its own special markings. The older pieces of pewter are rare and costly and, in most instances, are housed in museums. However, it is not difficult or costly to form a collection covering the past 200 years. Material can still be found. Handle pewter carefully. It is soft and dents easily.

Photographs

The hobby of collecting photographs is a very interesting pursuit. Collectors have many specialized fields from which to choose. Entire collections are made up of old photographs of politicians, actors and actresses, the sea, or mountain scenery. In general, this is a fairly inexpensive hobby.

Pianos

The collector of pianos seeks either the instrument itself or the nameplate inscription that is placed over the keyboard. Our modern pianos evolved gradually, starting with the monochord and clavichord of the early 17th century. These have a soft, hesitating tone. Next came the Spinet (also 17th century) which has a small volume and is generally incapable of dynamic modification by differences in touch. The most important key instrument of the 18th century was the harpischord. In form and arrangement, it resembles a grand piano, however it lacks an expressive character through touch. Mozart was fond of another early type of piano, the Viennese pianoforte of the 18th century. The 19th century introduced new mechanisms to provide even greater volume and tonal color. One of the first Steinway pianos is now the property of The National Gallery in Washington, D.C. The beauty of the wood, design style, and decorations on the piano greatly influence value. Collecting pianos is something like collecting elephants—it's expensive and requires considerable space for display.

Picture Frames

Sometimes the only value of a painting is its frame. If it is in good repair, the frame can be cut down to a usable size. All kinds of frames from late 19th century to Art Deco may have value.

Pin Cushions

These originated in medieval days. The earliest examples were wrapped cylinders made of silver, ivory, and wood to protect hand-wrought iron pins. Pin cushions of the 17th to 19th centuries were often flat and in the design of dolls, birds, vegetables, fruit, and common household objects. There is an innumerable variety of styles and sizes. Emery filling was used to sharpen points and to remove rust.

Pipes

Ancient pipes are considered those used by American aborigines. These old Indian pipes are found in the mounds, camps, and burial grounds of the Indians from centuries ago. Pipes of beautiful workmanship have also been left to us by the ancient Aztec Indians of Mexico. The most famous of all Indian pipes is the pipe of peace called the "Calumet". The ordinary pipe generally was adorned by a carved figure in the form of a wolf, bear, fish, beaver, otter, etc. But collectors beware—many modern Indian pipes imitate these antique styles. Early pipes were made of stone (usually red pipestone) and clay. After Sir Walter Raleigh introduced tobacco to the Old World, pipe smoking became popular in England and spread throughout the world. Pipes from this period usually had a hallmark on the bottom of the bowl and were often dated. The Dudeen of Ireland and the Cutty Pipe of Scotland are both examples of the early English clay pipe. Occasionally a wood or silver pipe is discovered that was used during this period, but these are rare. The early French clay pipes are most attractive and show up nicely in a collection. The bowls were carved in many styles of liberty and in Grecian motifs. Grotesque figures, steam engines, death's heads, and animals are but a few of the French clays that are collected. The long-stemmed German burgermeister painted porcelains, and Hungarian cherry wood silver-trimmed pipes are popular with collectors. The Chinese water pipe, the Turkish hookah, the Egyptian skidoo, and the old Japanese small bowl pipes all give an exotic touch to a collection. Opium pipes may also be included under this heading. The now famous corncob pipe has taken the place of the old clay pipe, and the gentleman's long-stemmed clays that are so often illustrated in old sporting prints have been replaced by the fine meerschaum and briars of today. Other types of pipes made from various kinds of wood, novel shapes, and miniatures are also included in collections. For the collector of pipes, material is available and not expensive. This type of hobby needs wall space for display or a cabinet to house the collection.

Pirate Relics

The search for original documents, treasure chests, cutlasses, pistols, and boarding axes has led collectors of this hobby into remote and dangerous places around the globe. Pirate enthusiasts have traveled to the icy north, through dense jungles, over impassable mountains, and to the bottom of the ocean to find their "stolen" treasures. Collecting relics of pirates is surely an exciting, romantic, and expensive hobby.

Pitchers

Pitchers of all sizes, styles, and shapes are now much sought after and used for decorative purposes. Many kinds of pitchers can be collected, so many in fact that many people specialize in a single type. In size they range from a huge pitcher used as a water and wine container to a pitcher as small as a thumbnail. Pitchers are also collected by their countries or continents of origin. Other collections are formed by collecting by material, such as glass, silver, china, pewter, etc. Some pitchers can be purchased for under a dollar while others, because of their age or exceptionally fine decoration, are priceless. Much material is available for the collector of this hobby. A collection of this type may be assembled at very little cost, or as costly as the collector desires it to be.

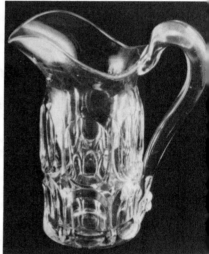

Staffordshire pitcher, left. Glass pitcher, c. 1857, found on Holy Island in the North Sea, below. Photographed by author.

Playing Cards

It is not known who invented playing cards. Certain kinds of playing cards were used in ancient Egypt, China, and India. The exact date of their introduction in Europe is not known, although they were used and enjoyed in medieval times. It is believed that the Crusaders found cards in the Orient and were the first Europeans to use them. The earliest existing cards were called tarot cards and were used by the Gypsies for fortune telling. The history and development of our modern playing cards is an adaptation of these old tarot cards. According to some authorities, the four kings represent the four ancient monarchies of the Jews, Greeks, Romans, and Franks. The suit marks represent the clergy (hearts), the nobility (spades), the serfs (clubs), and the citizens (diamonds). Excise tax marks may appear over the ace of spades in cards dating from 1712 to 1862. Until 1840, the backs were usually plain. Rounded corners first appeared in 1862. Many modern decks of cards show commemorative designs and views, both on face and back. For the person interested in this hobby, material is still available. The collecting of playing cards as a hobby is a classical one—it is not difficult to store and has a continuing interest as gambling seems to be inherent in the human species. Visit antique shops, look in old trunks and in attics, and you may be rewarded by a find.

Porcelain

The word "porcelain" is quite often applied to all the delicate and finer varieties of china. This is not entirely accurate as porcelain should only be associated with specific types of ceramic. Since the dawn of civilization, much work was carried out in the European and Asian countries to perfect the art of pottery. In the Far East, the Chinese developed an exquisite white translucent porcelain from their glazed and hand-fired pottery. Chinese porcelain became the wonder of the medieval world. This type of porcelain became a connecting link between pottery and glass, due to its translucent qualities and delicate composition. Much trading went on between countries and continents for experimental and useful purposes. England made a vast improvement on its porcelain by adding powdered ox bones to the other ingredients. Today English bone china is considered among the finest. The 20th century opened with an immensely broader outlook among the potters of Europe and America. Taste, skill, and all sorts of improvements were brought forth to create porcelain as it is today. Some of the finest and best known types of porcelain are the Ming and the Sung porcelain of China, English bone china, the Florentine ware, the Dresden china of Germany, and the Sevres and Limoges of France. When buying porcelain pieces, check for marks of the manufacturer or artisan. To gain value of the years, porcelain must be flawless. Cracks, chips, or worn glaze reduce value. Complete sets are more valuable than individual pieces.

Postcards

Postcard collecting can be interesting, and educational. The geographical story of the world can be told in picture form on these cards. Furthermore, all types of subjects have formed dandy postcard collections—plants, animals, land formations, sports, major events (such as the Chicago World's Fair in 1892-93), famous people (the Roosevelt family), humorous cards, and of course, postcards of scenery from different locations around the globe. Postcards reproducing photographs by well-known artists or photographers make another kind of collection. In addition, there are many beautiful examples of designers' and printers' art issued on postcards. Silk, tinsel, wood, and leather have also been used to manufacture postcards. By the way, contrary to popular belief, authentically old postcards showing erotic pictures are very rare indeed; at the time it was against the law in America to print or send such postcards through the mail. The hobby of collecting postcards is one that is within the reach of all. It is not an expensive hobby and much knowledge can be gained from it. All that is required is a display album.

Pottery

The word "pottery" generally includes all objects made from clay and hardened by fire. Another definition might be "any ceramic ware other than porcelain." Pottery is dependent on two important properties: the composition of the clay, and the techniques used when the clay is fired. The clays found on or near the surface of the

Irish porcelain cup and saucer, c. 1882-1892, top left. Early 19th century Straffordshire platters, center. "Mendenhall Ferry," appraised at $260 (bottom left). "Sandusky, Ohio," appraised at $475 (bottom right). "Detroit," appraised $240 (top). A pair of 18th century porcelain jardinieres, decorated in relief with blooming Prunus trees and birds and coated with a white glaze, extreme left. Two 18th century Meissen porcelain figurines, extreme right.

earth are numerous and have different compositions. The varieties have led to diverse qualities of potteries from different countries. The degree of heat used for firing (baking in a kiln) and the length of time the clay is baked will produce different types of pottery. Pottery varies in plasticity, hardness, texture, color, and even odor. Today, the white firing—clays of southern England are transported throughout the world for manufacturing of modern wares. Of course, as late as the 18th century, potters could only use clays of their own surrounding district. For the collector, there is a vast supply of knowledge available. The main source is the antiques shop. Old manufacturing companies, both abroad and locally, are other sources. Each country has certain distinctive pieces: Kwang-Yao and Yu Hsing Yao of China, the Byzantine ware of Egypt, Majolica and Samian ware of Italy, and Palissy and Henri Deux ware of France.

Twenty-eight-inch T'ang pottery horse, c. 618-907 A.D., with traces of polychrome.

Prints

An original print is the image of paper or similar material made by one or more processes, commonly known as woodcut, lithograph, and silkscreen. The process allows for more than one impression of each image. Therefore an original print does not mean it is unique. The total number of prints made of one image is an edition. A number may appear on the print, such as 5/25, meaning this is the fifth example in a total edition of 25. Very large editions are not as valuable, particularly when they are intended for commercial purposes. The collecting of prints is centuries old and one of the most fascinating types of hobbies. The earliest known engraving dates back to 1446. From this date to the early 16th century, most of the engraved work was done in Italy, the Netherlands, and Germany. Albrecht Durer (1471-1528) is considered to be the supreme master of this art form. The greatest genius in the art of etching is Rembrandt (17th century). Since his time, there have been many artists of note, but it remained for James McNeill Whistler, who worked in the late 19th century, to become the first great modern etcher. He inspired new interest in this form of expression that has enjoyed increasing collector demand. Colored lithograph prints, such as those published by Currier and Ives, are very popular today. As a hobby, the forming of a print collection is intriguing and uplifting.

Quilts

Quilting is made by stitching together two layers of fabric often with an interlining, forming patterns in low relief. Earliest quilting was used in garments. Bed quilts have recently become recognized as works of art. Values are set by the brightness of the colors, the intricacies of the patterns and originality of design. Amish and Mennonite patchwork quilts appliqued in small-pieced patterns are very costly. Although condition is a major factor, age isn't. The pastel quilts of the 1930's can sometimes be bought for under $100.

Railroads

A collection of this hobby can consist of old timetables, tickets, newspapers, stamps, pictures, freight bills, books, models, and parts of railroad equipment. From the days of George Stephenson's locomotive, the Rocket (1829), made for the Liverpool and Manchester Railway, to the first United States transcontinental train of the Northern Pacific Railroad, to the present-day Tres Grande Vitesse trains of the French National Railway, the story of the railroad is the story of commercial growth. Much material is available that will permit a collection large enough to outfit a museum or small enough to fit into an album.

Rugs

Oriental—Buying an antique oriental rug is a complex business. Look for aesthetic design and brilliance of colors. Check for worn areas and dry rot. (Bend an edge—if it's brittle and cracks, that's dry rot.) Prices can go sky-high for an original of excellent quality.

Braided—These are favorites today. Look for durability by buying rugs made only of 100% wool. Beware of obvious or broken lacing threads.

Hooked—Made from rags, hooked rugs dating from 1840 to 1860 are very popular now. Look for free-style designs of pastoral scenes, plants, or animals. The real thing has a rough, textured surface due to the variety of fabrics used. A small hooked rug suitable as a wall hanging can be had at a reasonable price.

Scent Bottles

Filled with either perfumed waters or smelling salts, scent bottles were extremely popular during the 18th and 19th centuries. These were made from porcelain, bone china, stoneware, glass, silver, painted enamels, and a variety of other materials. Styles included many imaginative shapes.

Silver

Pure silver is shimmering white, lustrous, soft, and ductile. Silver is usually alloyed with other metals such as copper to add hardness. Know hallmarks and design periods; each country and town possesses individual marks for identification and for determining silver alloy. Fine silver is .950 or 95% pure; sterling silver is .925 or 92.5% pure; and continental is .800 or 80% pure. Silver is also used to "coat" less expensive metals in processes known as Sheffield plate and electroplate. Silver is valued to some extent by weight; therefore, the more physical weight a piece of silver has, the more valuable the item. Be alerted that certain items, like candlesticks, may be weighted with lead or resin for stability. Silverplate is obviously not as valuable and does not wear as well. Well-known brands or silversmiths add value. Silver dents easily, so watch for condition.

Snuff Boxes

The collector of snuff boxes is fortunate in this hobby. Collections can be assembled no matter what size the pocketbook, as snuff boxes were made out of everything from tin and wood to brass, gold, and silver, and were sometimes studded with precious jewels. The old Brazilian Indians were the discoverers of snuff. Their snuff boxes were made of bone or wood and were decorated similarly to old Inca designs, which showed the human body or animal figure in grotesque forms. East Indians later on used snuff boxes that were hollow and pear shaped, carved from ebony or other hard wood. The Moors used hollowed bamboo sticks, the ends stuffed with cork, for their snuff boxes. The Chinese used a snuff bottle similar in appearance to a scent bottle. These were beautifully carved of amber, malachite, turquoise, jade, and agate. This type of snuff bottle is among the rarities of this hobby. Snuff boxes used by important persons of years ago are particularly valuable, such as the snuff box of Catherine the II of Russia or the snuff boxes of Louis XIV, and are examples of precious metal and bejeweled snuff boxes. Snuff boxes have been made in many curious shapes— slippers, drums, harpsichords, snakes, coffins, boats, even a hen sitting on her nest. Many beautiful boxes were made of Dresden china. Bone, wood, tortoise shell, lacquer, and the commoner metals were all used to manufacture snuff boxes.

Speakeasy Cards

Speakeasy cards are exquisite souvenirs of Americana, one of the few visible reminders of the experiment called Prohibition. Bootleggers, hijackers, gun men and their molls, bloodshed and crime—these are all vividly brought to mind by these small pasteboards that were speakeasy cards. Those of infamous clubs or signed by mobsters such as Al Capone are most desirable. Material for a collection of these cards is still available. However, they are scarce — most people threw them out when liquor was legalized.

Stamps

A tremendous category for collectors is postage stamps. Beyond their financial possibilities, stamp collecting is an interesting educational tool to learn about geography, animals, flowers, historic events, and notable people. Opinions vary on whether stamps should be cancelled or uncancelled. In certain instances, they're more valuable when cancelled because in recent times, stamps have been generated for the purposes of fundraising and tax shelters. If the stamp was never really used, I do not consider it as a valuable collectible. There are people who trade them, but that does not make them worthwhile investments for the future. A local stamp that was really used has greater value. Condition is extremely important. The illustration should be well centered; the stamp should have its original glue; and the perforations should extend all around the stamp. Of course, some "imperfect" stamps, such as those with inverted pictures or misprints, are extremely valuable because they are so rare.

Thimbles

Commonly made of bronze, thimbles were first used by the ancient Romans. Medieval thimbles were often made from stitched leather, brass, or steel. From the mid-16th century on, thimbles became ornate, made of precious metals and often with a motto on the rim. By the 18th century, thimbles came with jewelled rims and exquisitely painted enamels. In the 19th century, popular materials included silver, bone china, ivory, jade, mother-of-pearl, and wood.

Bogus stamps from the author's father's collection. ▶

Bogus

PARAGUAY   CANCELLATION   BRUNEI

SEDANG   CHRISTMAS IS.   MOZAMBIQUE

CHANGELING   SURCHARGE CANCELLATION   FIG. 1   GUATEMALA

COUNTERFEIT

MADE TO DEFRAUD
THE GOVERNMENT.

Tools

Whether for use or decorative display, antique tools are fairly affordable. Popular examples include a carpenter's wood clamp, a cherrywood level, a folding rule, or an iron hatchet.

Toys

Antique and semi-antique toys are tremendously in demand, and high prices naturally follow. Turn of the century carved and painteded wooden hobby horses will cost well over several hundred dollars. Nineteenth century pull toys on wheels or cast iron automobiles can also be quite costly. A 1930's Felix the Cat on a scooter will sell for over $100.

Toy Soldiers

Nineteenth century lead soldiers are very popular now. Best names are Heyde (Germany) and Mignot (French). Complete sets are most valuable. Look for fine details marking an original. Reproductions are worth very little (especially if made of plastic). A complete set of solid lead soldiers in its original box will fetch several hundred dollars.

Valentines

The first commercial valentine on record to be sold was in 1761. Exchanging valentines is an ancient tradition, widely popular in the 19th century. During that period, valentines sent to a sweetheart were enclosed in beautifully embossed envelopes of lacelike patterns. The workmanship and design of these envelopes alone were so fine and original that lace makers today use them as models. Valentines are a tribute to St. Valentine, a martyred priest in Rome. Claudius the Cruel had issued a decree forbidding marriage, but St. Valentine defied it. While performing a wedding ceremony, he was dragged from before the altar and thrust into a prison where he languished until he died (presumably on February 14th). Before long, he was accepted as the patron saint of lovers. Early cards were of thin, folded paper with a printed verse and a hand-colored picture. The Victorians created elaborate designs by embossing, engraving, or lithography. Paper lace was a great favorite. Some valentines were quite complex with surprise pictures, transforming scenes, and artificial flowers that required no mere envelopes, but special boxes. There were also many more cheaply made valentines. Comic and vulgar cards can also be found. Some of the older valentines are very rare and valuable. Valentines are also found in many collections of Americana.

Valentine, c. 1930, from the NYHS Folk Arts Collection.

Violins

The instrument of romance, poetry, and love is the violin. Some of the greatest violin makers—the Amati family (Antonio, Hieronymus and Nicola), and the Guarneri family—were of the 16th and 17th centuries. Their violins are among the most sought after by collectors. But the dream of every violinist and violin collector is to own a Stradivarius. Antonio Stradivari (c.1644-1737), born in Cremona, Italy, is considered the greatest and finest violin maker who ever lived. Today his violins sell for well over $100,00. For every genuine Stradivarius, however, there are perhaps 10,000 copies, most made in Germany and France. These copies were not intended to deceive, but were made for purely commercial purposes over the past 200 years. These violins have a facsimile label indicating the Stradivarius model after which they are copied. Nonetheless, inexperienced buyers often mistake them as authentic. These old copies range in value from under $100 to several hundred dollars. The world's finest collections of violin masterpieces of the 16th, 17th, and 18th centuries are found primarily in museums. This is a hobby indulged in only by the very wealthy.

Wallpaper

Collecting both antique and modern wallpaper is a hobby which associates itself with a number of other interesting and instructive arts and sciences, such as the study of architecture, art, interior decorating, paper manufacturing, printing, color, and design. Some knowledge of these subjects is necessary for the collector in order to properly classify the papers. The origin of wallpaper is unknown. France, Holland, China, and Spain all contend for the honor. The first written record of wallpaper (originally called "chamber hangings") has been found in England. It was mentioned in the 1536 records of the Monastery of Saint Syxborough in the isle of Shepy in the county of Kent. Most types of early wallpaper were hand-painted or made by the wood block print method. These are rare and difficult to acquire. The collector is indeed lucky to possess a fragment of one of these old papers. In America, the serious minded Colonists were too intent on simply surviving to give much thought to wall decorations. It was not until the early 1700's that wallpaper was used, and was imported from England. The first wallpaper manufacturer on record in America is John Rugen, who had a factory in New York City. The wallpaper collector will meet with innumerable types of printing and design, from the simplest block patterns to exquisite scenic papers. Much material is still available. Papers can be displayed in an album.

Wooden Indians

From the time Sir Walter Raleigh brought tobacco and pipes back to England, the wooden Indian was the symbol of the tobacconist. During the middle of the late 19th century, different styles were introduced. The Indian brave and the Indian maid were the two most common figures. However, other non-Indian figures also graced the entrances to smoke shops. These included Scotch lassies, cupids, policemen, blacks, Punch's and Puck's, jockeys, baseball players, actors, soldiers, sailors, and even statues of Liberty. The traditional wooden Indian usually held a bunch of cigars or a cigar box in his hand. These were hand-carved, and in some instances, are very fine examples of this craft. They closely resemble figureheads of ships, and in fact, were sometimes made by the same master craftsmen. Wooden Indians were painted in bright and gaudy colors and were usually trimmed in genuine gold or silver leaf. For the collector of wooden Indians, the supply is limited to manufacturing concerns of the 19th century. They are no longer made, as specialized tobacco shops have all but disappeared. The only way to procure wooden Indians is from an antique dealer. The very fortunate may be able to pick one up from an old storekeeper. Today, wooden Indians are worth their weight in gold.

Index

ROTHSCHILD ON ANTIQUES & COLLECTIBLES

INDEX

Trade value, 12, 33, 35
Trendiness, 27

Utility of item, 24, 35, 71

Valentines, 156-157
Value, of collections, 5, 25-26, 50, 52, 84-85
Value of items, 46
  appraisals and, 44
  changes in, 11-13
  decreases in, 11, 76
  determining, 13, 16-35, 58-63

increases in, 11, 12, 76-81
money and, 12
resale, 78, 81-85
sentimental, 29, 35
Victorian jewelry, 135
Violins, 158

Wallpaper, 158-159
Wedgewood, 25
Wholesale value, 12, 16, 33-34, 35
Wooden Indians, 159
Woodwork, color of, 24

Bibliography

A BRIEF LIST OF REFERENCE RESOURCES FOR WORKS OF ART, ANTIQUES, AND COLLECTIBLES

I. IDENTIFYING THE ARTIST OR THE WORK:

Alsop, Joseph. *The Rare Art Traditions: A History of Art Collecting and Its Linked Phenomena Wherever They Have Appeared.* New York: Harper & Row, 1982.

Comprehensive serious history covering every aspect: sociological, psychological, economic, as well as aesthetic.

American Art Directory. Edited by Jaques Cattell Press. New York: Bowker. Updated biennially.

Data on art museums, libraries, associations, schools, and studios, including universities and colleges with art departments and museums, mainly for the United States and Canada.

Appletons' Cyclopaedia of American Biography. 6 vols. New York: Appleton, 1886.

Art World, The: A 75-Year Treasury of ARTnews. Edited by Barbaralee Diamondstein. New York: Rizzoli/ARTnews, 1977.

Lavishly illustrated history of the development of modern art.

167

Baigell, Matthew. *Dictionary of American Art.*

Information on important American painters, sculptors, printmakers, and photographers.

Benezeit, Emmanuel. *Dictionnaire critique et documentaire des peintres, sculpteurs, dessinateurs et graveurs.* 10 vols. Paris: Grund, 1976.

Biographical information on an enormous number of artists of all times and all countries. Many artists' signatures are illustrated. Some sales prices are given.

Bryan, Michael. *Dictionary of Painters and Engravers.* Reprint of 1905 ed. Port washington, N.Y.: Kennikat Press, 1964.

Quick source for lists of artists' works.

Caplan, H.H., ed. *Classified Directory of Artists' Signatures, Symbols, and Monograms.* 2nd ed. Detroit, Mich.: Gale Research Co., 1982.

Extensive cross-reference index enabling one to properly identify an artist by his mark regardless of legibility.

Catalogue of American Portraits. New York: New York Historical Society, 1941.

Complete Encyclopedia of Antiques, The. Compiled by *The Connoisseur.* L.G.G. Ramsay, ed. New York: Hawthorn, 1962.

Cummings, Paul, ed. *Dictionary of Contemporary American Artists.* 3rd ed. New York: St. Martin's Press, 1977.

Who's who in contemporary art.

Cyclopedia of Painters and Paintings. 4 vols. Edited by John Denison Champlin, Jr. New York: Scribner's, 1887.

Davenport's Art Reference & Price Guide. R. J. Davenport, 1986.

Dictionary of Greek and Roman Antiquities. New York: Harper & Brothers, 1881.

Edlin, Herbert L. *What Wood Is That? A Manual of Wood Identification.* New York: Viking, 1969.

BIBLIOGRAPHY

Encyclopedia of World Art. 15 vols. New York: McGraw-Hill, 1968.

Ensko, Stephen. G.C. *American Silversmiths and Their Marks II.* Robert Ensko, 1937.

Fielding, Mantle. *Dictionary of American Painters, Sculptors, and Engravers.* Edited by Glenn B. Opitz. Bridgeport, Conn.: Associated Booksellers, 1974.

Primarily late 19th- and early 20th-century artists, but does include artists of the 17th and 18th centuries.

Fine Art Reproduction of Old and Modern Masters. Greenwich, Conn.: New York Graphic Society, 1976.

An excellent handy reference source of color paintings.

Foster, J.J. *Dictionary of Painters and Miniatures, 1525-1850.* Burt Franklin, 1926. Reprinted by Somerset Publications.

Groce, George Cuthbert, and Wallace, David H. *The New York Historical Society's Dictionary of Artists in America, 1564-1860.* New Haven: Yale University Press, 1957.

Some 10,000 names of artistis active within the limits of the United States prior to 1869 are listed. Quite comprehensive.

Haggar, Reginald G. *A Dictionary of Art Terms.* New York: Hawthorn, 1962.

Art terms, movements, styles, techniques, materials, and abbreviations, covering architecture, sculpture, painting and the graphic arts.

Havlice, Patricia Pate. *Index to Artistic Biography.* 2 vols. Metuchen, N.J.: Scarecrow Press, 1973. First supplement, 1981.

Excellent reference source. Includes artist's name, nationality, media used, and localities.

Jackson, Sir Charles James. *English Goldsmiths and Their Marks.* Borden, 1921.

Janson, H.W. *History of Art: A Survey of the Major Visual Arts from the Dawn of History to the Present Day.* New York: Abrams, 1977.

Krause Chester, and Mishler, Clifford. *Standard Catalog of World Coins.* Krause Publications, 1985.

Lee, Cuthbert. *Early American Portrait Painters.* New Haven: Yale University Press, 1929.

Lindemann, Gottfried. *Prints and Drawings: A Pictorial History.* New York: Praeger, 1970.

Lipman, Jean, and Armstrong, Tom. *American Folk Painters of Three Centuries.* New York: Hudson Hills Press, 1980.

Lipman, Jean, and Winchester, Alice. *The Flowering of American Folk Art (1776-1976).* New York: Viking, 1974.

Lynes, Russell. *The Art Makers: An Informal History of Painting, Sculpture, and Architecture.* New York: Atheneum, 1970; reprinted by Dover, 1982.

MacDonald-Taylor, Margaret. *A Dictionary of Marks.* New York: State Mutual Books, 1981.

Maillard, Robert, ed. *New Dictionary of Modern Sculpture.* New York: L. Amiel Publications, 1971.
Biographical details, technical and stylistic information.

Mallet, Daniel T. *Mallet's Index of Artists; international-biographical; including painters, sculptors, illustrators, engravers and etchers of the past and present.* Originally published by R. R. Bowker. Reprinted by Peter Smith, 1948. Some inaccuracies, but this is a very good source for learning how much information about an artist is available.

New International Illustrated Encyclopedia of Art, The. 24 vols. Sir John Rothenstein, editorial consultant. Greystone Press, 1967.

Pearson, Katherine. *American Crafts: A Source Book for the Home.* New York: Stewart, Tabori & Chang, 1983.
Lavishly photographed all-color source book of fine contemporary crafts, covering clay, wood, fiber, metal, and glass. Advice on what to look for, how to collect and display. Fine glossary of craft terms and explanations of techniques.

BIBLIOGRAPHY

Phaidon Dictionary of Twentieth-Century Art. New York: Praeger, 1973.

Random House Collector's Encyclopedia, The: Victoriana to Art Deco. Introduction by Roy Strong. New York: Random House, 1974.

Richard, Lionel. *The Concise Encyclopedia of Expressionism,* Compact reference work on all aspects of Expressionism.

Serullaz, Maurice. *The Concise Encyclopedia of Impressionism.* Thieme, Ulrich, and Becker, Felix, eds. *Allgemeines Lexikon der Bildenden Kunstler von der Antike bis ur Gegenwart.* 37 vols. Somerset Publications, 1906-50.

Most complete and scholarly, with locations or artworks and lengthy bibliographies. A 6-volume supplement, edited by Hans Vollmer, published in 1953, covers artists of the 20th century.

Who's Who in American Art. New York: Bowker, published biennally from 1936 to the present.

II. IDENTIFYING THE ANTIQUE OR COLLECTIBLE:

Antiques Dealer. Clifton, N.J.: Ebel-Doctorow Publications, Inc.

Monthly magazine of the antiques business.

Aronson, Joseph. *Encyclopedia of Furniture.* New York: Crown, 1965.

Compendium of furniture styles through the 19th century including definitions, descriptions, illustrations, sketches giving details of construction and design.

Art & Antique. Bergenfield, N.J. (monthly).

Art & Auction. New York (monthly).

Antique Collector, The. London (monthly).

ARTnews. New York (monthly).

Battison, Edward A., and Kane, Patricia E. *The American Clock, 1725-1865.* Greenwich, Conn.: New York Graphic Society, 1973.

Blodgett, Richard. *Photographs: A Collector's Guide.* New York: Ballantine Books, 1979.
A definitive reference book on buying fine photographs, with detailed information about prices, dealers, and auctions, and an introduction to hundreds of photographers from 1839 to the present.

Bracegirdle, C.A. *First Book of Antiques.* London: Heinemann, 1970.

Brener, C. *The Underground Collector.* New York: Simon & Schuster, 1970.

Britten's Old Clocks and Watches and Their Makers. New York: Charles River Books, 1976.
Historical and descriptive account of the different styles of clocks and watches of the past in England and abroad containing a list of nearly 14,000 makers; lavishly illustrated.

Clark, Garth R., and Hughto, Margie. *A Century of Ceramics in the United States, 1879-1979.* New York: Dutton, 1979. Illustrated anthology on ceramic art.

Chaffers, William. *Marks and Monograms on European and Oriental Pottery and Porcelain.* 2 vols. London: William Reeves.
Authoritative historical survey of British, European, and Oriental marks and monograms.

Comstock, Helen. *American Furniture: Seventeenth, Eighteenth, and Nineteenth Century Styles.* Exton, Pa.: Schiffer, 1980.

Concise Encyclopedia of American Antiques, The. Edited by Helen Comstock. New York: Hawthorn, 1969.
A very useful book, lavishly illustrated, ranging from furniture, silver, pewter, cooper, brass, period styles, pottery, porcelain, glass, needlework, buttons, playing cards, firearms, folk painting, miniatures, toys, etc.

Cowie, D. *Antiques: How to Identify and Collect Them.* Yoseloff, 1971.

BIBLIOGRAPHY

Crawley, W. *A Guide to the Identification of 18th-Century English Furniture.* New York: Hart Publishing Co., 1972.

Daniel, Dorothy. *Cut and Engraved Glass, 1771-1905* (The Collectors Guide to American Wares). New York: M. Barrows. 1950.

Davenport, Millia. *The Book of Costume.* New York: Crown, 1964.
A definitive history of costume which can be applied to identifying paintings and portraits as to period and style.

Drepperd, Carl W. *American Pioneer Arts & Artists.* Springfield, Mass.: The Pond-Ekberg Co., 1942.

Edwards, Ralph. *Sheraton Furniture Design.* Central Islip. N.Y.: Transatlantic Arts, Inc., 1974.

_____. *English Chairs.* New York: State Mutual Books, 1970.

Encyclopedia of Antiques, An. Harold Lewis Bond. Gale, 1975.
Faxon, Alicia Craig. *Collecting Art on a Shoestring.* New York: Barre Publishing Co., 1969.

Florence, Gene. *The Collector's Encyclopedia of Depression Glass Collector Books.* Paducah, Ky.
Descriptions and color illustrations for many types of Depression glass.

Freeman, Larry. *Grand Old American Bottles.* Watkins Glen, N.Y.: Century House, 1964.
Lists glass bottle types (liquor, medicine, etc.) from colonial days to the present with lavish illustrations.

Garner, Sir Harry. *Chinese and Japanese Cloisonne Enamels.* Rutland, Vt.: C. E. Tuttle, 1962.
Scholarly and comprehensive guide, profusely illustrated.

Guide to Art Reference Books. Compiled by Mary W. Chamberlin. Chicago: American Library Association, 1959. Comprehensive guide to art reference books.

Haslam, Malcom. *Marks and Monograms of the Modern Movement, 1875-1930.* New York: Scribner & Sons, 1977.

Guide to the marks and monograms of European decorative artists, craftsmen, and manufacturers in the fields of glass, ceramics, metalwork, jewelry, graphics, furniture, and textiles.

Hawley, Walter A. *Oriental Rugs, Antique and Modern.* New York: Peter Smith & Dover, 1970.

Very useful and accurately and intelligently assembled.

Head, R. E. *The Lace and Embroidery Collector.* Reprint of 1922 edition, Gale, 1971.

Hornung, Clarence P. *Treasury of American Design.* 2 vols. New York: Abrams, 1972.

Lavishly illustrated compendium of articles of daily use and adornment in this country from early colonial times to the close of the 19th century. Based on the Index of American Design at the National Gallery of Art.

———. *Treasury of American Antiques.* New York: Abrams, 1977.

———, compiler. *A Source Book of Antiques and Jewelry Designs.* New York: Da Capo Press, 1977.

Hudson, Norman. *Antiques Illustrated and Priced.* Thomas Yoseloff, 1978.

Contains more than 2,000 illustrations of furniture, lighting devices, paintings, household items, and prints, with dated prices.

Ketchum, William. *The Catalog of American Antiques.* New York: Rutledge Books, 1977.

Illustrated guide for identification and dated prices of major categories of American antiques.

Kovel, Ralph, and Kovel, Terry. *The Kovel's Collector's Guide to American Art Pottery.* New York: Crown, 1974.

Describes makers, artists, dates, marks, and lines of American art pottery.

BIBLIOGRAPHY

Latham, Jean. *Collecting Miniature Antiques*. New York: Scribner's, 1972.

Luckey, Carl F. *Official Price Guide to Silver, Silverplate and Their Makers, 1865-1920*. Florence, Ala.: House of Collectibles.
All types of silver from candlesticks to ink bottles. Illustrated profusely.

Lysman, J.H., compiler. *The Collector in America*. Studio Publications, 1971.

MacDonald-Taylor, Margaret, ed. *A Dictionary of Marks*. New York: State Mutual Books, 1981.
A comprehensive one-volume identification handbook for antique collectors of furniture, metalwork, tapestry, and ceramics.

Mackay, J. *A Guide for Collectors and Investors*. Antiques of the Future. New York: Studio Vista, 1970.

Mason, Anita. *An Illustrated Dictionary of Jewelry*. New York: Harper & Row, 1974.
Covers gemstone identification, techniques of jewelry manufacturing, history of jewelry, hallmarking and more.

McKearin, George S., and McKearin, Helen. *American Glass*. New York: Crown, 1941

Mebane, J. *The Complete Book of Collecting Art Nouveau*. New York: Coward-McCann, 1970.

Miller, Edgar G., Jr. *American Antique Furniture: A Book for Amateurs*. 2 vols. New York: Dever, 1966.
Practical guide to the identification of American antique furniture of all styles and periods prior to 1840.

Neustadt, Egon. *The Lamps of Tiffany*. New York: Fairfield Press, 1970.
Comprehensive survey of Tiffany lamps, with magnificent color plates.

Newman, Harold. *An Illustrated Dictionary of Glass.* London: Thames and Hudson, 1978.

A comprehensive guide to styles, terms, regions, and individuals involved in glassmaking from prehistoric times to the present.

Nutting, Wallace. *The Clock Book.* Gale, 1975.

Description of foreign and American antique clocks and a list of their makers. Profusely illustrated.

Pistolese, Rosana, and Horsting, Ruth. *History of Fashions.* New York: Wiley, 1970.

Raycraft, D. R. *Early American Folk and Country Antiques.* Ruthland, Vt.: C.E. Tuttle, 1971.

Revi, Albert Christian. *American Art Nouveau Glass.* Exton, Pa.: Schiffer, 1981.

American glass objects by such makers as Tiffany, Nash, Durand, Steuben. Beautifully illustrated.

_____. *American Cut and Engraved Glass.* Exton, Pa.: Schiffer, 1982.

Clear photographs and precise line drawings of pieces, trademarks, and labels, beginning with the development of the cut-glass industry in America.

_____. Nineteenth Century Glass. Exton, Pa.: Schiffer, 1981.

Traces the development and refinement of glassmaking throughout the 19th century. Fully illustrated with photographs (some in color) and line drawings.

Sack, Albert. *Fine Points of Furniture: Early America.* New York: Crown, 1982.

Compares merits and values of more than 100 types of Early American furniture. Abundantly illustrated.

Towner, W. *The Elegant Auctioneers.* New York: Hill & Wang.

BIBLIOGRAPHY

Voss, Thomas M. *Antique American Country Furniture: A Field Guide.* New York: Harper & Row, 1978.

Information on dating, authenticating, and construction of American country furniture.

Woodhouse, Charles P. *The Victoriana Collector's Handbook.* G. Bell, 1970.

Worrell, Estelle. *American Costume: 1840-1920.* Harrisburg, Pa.: Stackpole, 1970.

A colorful history of styles from buckskins to bloomers, arranged chronologically and cross-referenced. Invaluable aid in dating portraits, painting, and other artwork.

Wyler, Seymour B. *Book of Old Silver: English, American, Foreign.* New York: Crown, 1937.

This illustrated history and guide to old silver includes a comprehensive table of hallmarks and information on how to buy and collect.

III. EVALUATING THE WORK OR THE ITEMS:

Andrews, John. *The Price Guide to Antique Furniture.*

Antique Collectors, 1979.

Extremely helpful to the collector who wants to learn about furniture available in shops, auctions, and antique fairs rather than the unobtainable museum quality pieces.

_____. *The Price Guide to Victorian, Edwardian, and 1920s Furniture.* Antique Collectors, 1980.

Identifies the complexities and copies of styles.

Gordon's Print Price Annual. New York: Martin Gordon, Inc.: published yearly.

International Auction Records. Compiled by Enrique Mayer. Vol. 1, 1967. Editions E.M.—Publisol, London, etc.

Annual editions quote prices collected at principal auctions in the United States and abroad. Works classified according to technique: engravings, drawing, watercolors, painting, sculpture. All prices quoted in dollars.

Lyle Official Antiques Review, 1984, The. Over 6,500 illustrations in over 250 categories of collecting, all priced in U.S. dollars and British pounds.

Price Guide to Collectable Antiques, The. Antique Collectors, 1979.

Price Guide to More Collectable Antiques, The. Antique Collectors, 1980.

Printworld Directory of Contemporary Prints and Prices, The. Selma Smith, editor/publisher. Bala Cynwyd, Pa.: Printworld, Inc.

Woodhouse, Charles P. *Investment in Art and Antiques.* G. Bell, 1969.